NO, YOU CAN'T BE AN ASTRONAUT

PATIENCE FAIRWEATHER, PHD

Copyright © 2020 Patience Fairweather

ISBN: 978-1-943476-63-3

Library of Congress Control Number: 2019950090

Cover and interior graphical elements by Freepik and Vecteezy.

DEDICATION

This book was inspired by my students.
I hope it helps.

CONTENTS

ACKNOWLEDGMENTS

Thanks to family, friends, colleagues, and indefatigable researchers whose work informs this book.

1. HOUSTON, WE HAVE A PROBLEM

John did everything right.

He went to college right after high school, to the most exclusive place he could get into—a big-name research university with Nobel laureates on the faculty. He had heard about the crisis-level shortage of STEM (Science, Technology, Engineering, and Mathematics) majors [1], so he chose to major in environmental science.

John wanted to graduate in four years, so he concentrated on his schoolwork. He turned down opportunities for internships and study abroad, as they would have lengthened his time to degree. He never met any of those Nobel laureates on the faculty. They worked mainly with graduate students, it turned out; undergraduates like John never saw them.

John graduated with a decent GPA and expected to earn enough to pay off his student loans quickly. Unfortunately, competition for the few desirable jobs was fierce, and many vacant positions were in remote areas. They offered no moving allowance or job security, and the pay was disappointingly low. John found his situation wasn't unique; 29% of graduates in his field were working part-time, and over half were in jobs that didn't require a college degree at all [2].

After a few months of job-hunting, John was out of money and options. He now works a part-time job. His employer limits his hours to avoid paying benefits. He can't get another degree now; not only can he not afford the tuition, but he's now one of the 80% of hourly workers with an unpredictable on-call work schedule, which prevents him from being able to attend classes [3]. He could get an additional degree online, but he's not sure it would be a wise investment. Online education isn't as well-respected as its traditional face-to-face counterpart [4, 5].

Fortunately, his parents are keeping him on their health insurance...for now.

John's story is not unusual. Although fewer than five percent of recent college graduates are unemployed, an additional 41 percent work in jobs that typically don't require a college degree [6]. And as he found, it's not just the much-maligned art history (56%) or ethnic studies (50%) majors who are taking your coffee order or folding shirts at the mall. 73% of criminal justice majors and 60% of business management majors are working in positions that typically don't require a college degree.

And it turns out there wasn't really a shortage of STEM workers after all. While politicians and pundits were banging on about the need for more STEM graduates, the evidence showed that the "STEM shortage" is largely a myth. Schools in the U.S. churn out more STEM graduates than there are available jobs, leading to oversupply in some fields [1, 7, 8].

HOW DID WE GET HERE?

The college degree used to be rare. In 1950, only six percent of U.S. adults over 25 had a four-year degree or higher. It was a credential that really stood out. But today, around one-third of U.S. adults over 25 have a four-year degree or higher. The college degree today is about as common as a high school diploma was in 1950 [9].

Now philanthropists and policymakers are pushing to get even more people to go to college [10], aiming to have up to 60% of the population holding a postsecondary degree [11]. Supporters of increased rates of college degree attainment cite the fact that people with college degrees earn more, on average, than people without them [12]. The claim is then made that increasing the number of college graduates will result in improved wages for graduates and non-graduates alike. This rests on two assumptions:

1) The demand for college graduates will rise to meet the supply, and
2) There are enough "good" (high-paying, stable) jobs out there to absorb the increased output of college graduates.

The first assumption is correct. Given a choice between two applicants, employers prefer the more-qualified candidate. What this means is that companies will now hire college graduates for jobs that used to require only a high school diploma. That's the source of the college premium: College graduates are filling the jobs that high school graduates used to get [13].

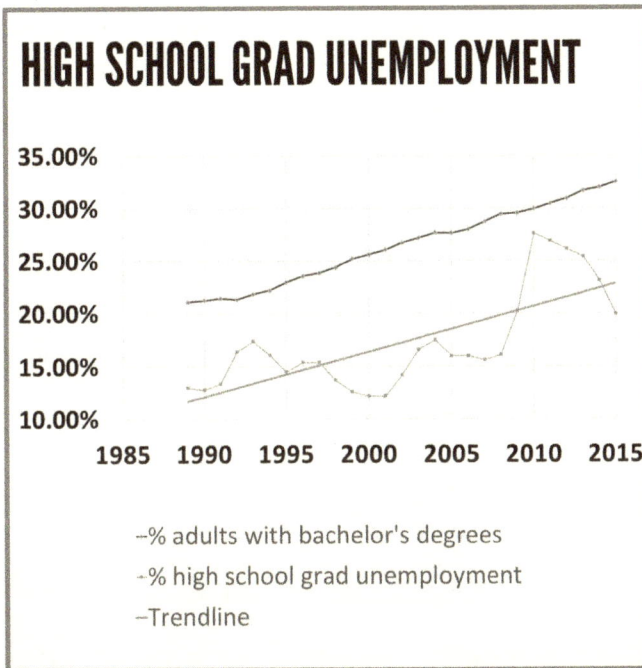

HIGH SCHOOL GRAD UNEMPLOYMENT

--% adults with bachelor's degrees
-•% high school grad unemployment
--Trendline

Unemployment among those with high school only has gone up at the same rate as college attainment. Sources: www.epi.org/publication/the-class-of-2015/ and nces.ed.gov/programs/digest/d15/tables/dt15_104.10.asp

7

Increasing the number of college graduates has not coincided with an increase in good jobs for those graduates; in fact, the opposite has happened. Since 1980 average income has decreased, the number of poverty-wage jobs has grown, and the percentage of jobs that are temporary or on-call has gone up [14].

Claims of an undersupply of college graduates have been contradicted by the evidence. For example, a 2010 Center on Education and the Workforce study projected that by 2018, 33% of all job openings would require a bachelor's degree or higher, while an additional 30% would require some postsecondary education [15].

As of 2019, according to the Department of Labor, only 21% of jobs in the United States required a bachelor's degree, and an additional 11% required an associate's degree, certificate, or some college. 63% of jobs required a high school diploma or less [16, 17].

Producing more college degrees hasn't produced more high-paying jobs. The defining problem in the U.S. job market isn't a skills gap; it's that too many educated people are chasing too few jobs [18]. As education levels have increased, the poor have simply become better-educated [19, 20].

How did the CEW researchers get a result so at odds with the Department of Labor? The researchers got their results by assuming underemployment doesn't exist. They define the size of the college labor market as a function of the number of college graduates currently employed in a given occupation [21]. For example, if 15% of taxi drivers have bachelor's degrees [22], that means 15% of taxi driver jobs *need* bachelor's degrees [21]. Had the study been submitted to a peer-reviewed journal, this unorthodox methodology might not have survived to publication.

Why advocate increasing college-going rates in a labor market that already has an oversupply of college graduates? A cynic might point to the fact that the Center on Education and the Workforce and similar college completion efforts are funded by the

Lumina Foundation for Education [23, 24], which has roots in the student-loan industry. When the nation's largest administrator of private student loans sold its assets to Sallie Mae, the Lumina Foundation was created with the proceeds, and former Sallie Mae board members have served as directors of Lumina [25]. The Lumina Foundation's stated goal is "increasing the proportion of Americans with high-quality degrees, certificates and other credentials to 60 percent by 2025" [26]. In light of this history, Lumina's relentless efforts to increase college enrollment could be seen as a conflict of interest [27]. But the college completion agenda is appealing even to those without ties to the student loan industry. Increased college attainment is an easily-understood, feel-good goal that allows us to ignore thorny structural issues.

Another reason to encourage everyone to go to college is that as the college degree has become more common, there is an increasing penalty for *not* having one. The college degree has come to be seen as necessary, but not sufficient [28].

VALUABLE BECAUSE THEY'RE RARE

It can be argued that college degrees in the job market are a *positional good* [29]. A *positional good* is defined as something that is valuable because it is scarce—the more people have it, the less it's worth [30]. What we see happening in the labor market seems to support this view. Employers in the United

States aren't offering more good jobs to accommodate the increased number of college graduates; instead, they're requiring college degrees for the jobs that used to go to high school grads [31].

Individually, chances are you're better off with a degree than without one (setting aside for the moment the chance that you might start college but not finish, ending up with debt and no degree [32]). But collectively, as more people earn college degrees, the less likely the average graduate is to attain a "good" job. There is now an oversupply of college degrees. A college degree is not a golden ticket; it's more like a hunting license.

People vs. Jobs

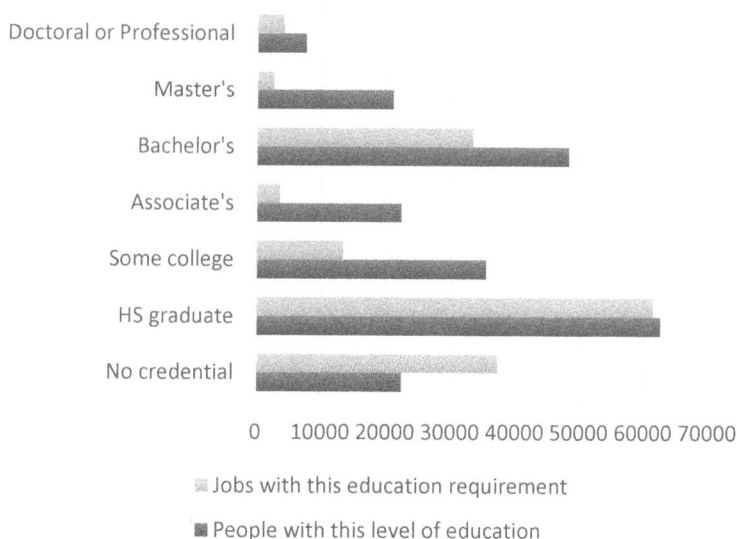

Sources:
https://www.census.gov/data/tables/2018/demo/education-attainment/cps-detailed-tables.html and
https://www.bls.gov/spotlight/2019/education-projections/home.htm
Numbers in thousands. Civilian noninstitutionalized population over 25.

For more on whether the value of a college education lies in the skills it imparts versus the signal it sends to employers, look up the "Sheepskin Effect."

WHY DIDN'T ANYONE TELL ME HOW HARD IT IS TO FIND A GOOD JOB?

Your counselors probably never told you that we have an oversupply of educated job-seekers. That's probably because no one told them. On the contrary, the career-advice industry is brimming with positivity. There's no shortage of books, inspirational posters, and desk plaques claiming that you that with the right attitude you can get paid for doing what you love. Why settle for a mere job, the gift-shop gurus ask, when you can follow your calling and fulfill your destiny?

"Shoot for the moon. Even if you miss, you'll land among the stars."

"Have the courage to follow your heart."

"Stop looking forward to Fridays and start looking forward to Mondays!"

"Do what you love and you'll never work a day in your life!"

Some unhelpful adages. Source: Your school counselor

This kind of advice is meant to be encouraging, and for some people it may be. But what if you don't have a particular passion that you yearn to pursue twenty hours a day? Are you a bad person if you actually do look forward to Fridays more than you look forward to Mondays? And are you the only one who's noticed that if you "land among the stars" you are then "adrift in outer space?"

WHAT'S WRONG WITH FOLLOWING YOUR PASSION?

Nothing at all—as long as you don't expect to get paid for it. Because as individual and unique as you undoubtedly are, your "passion" is probably the same as a lot of other people's. As life coach Gabrielle Loehr observes, "not everyone's passion can turn into a paying job and your bills are not going to pay themselves [33]."

Here are the numbers: Most professional writers earn less than a thousand dollars a year from their writing [34]. Fewer than one in 500 high school athletes ends up playing professionally; for basketball players it's fewer than one in 10,000 [35]. And astronauts? NASA takes fewer than 1% of applicants [36]. And if you're thinking about going into movies or politics, your chances aren't much better. [37].

YOU'RE MORE LIKELY TO DIE IN THE TUB THAN MAKE IT IN HOLLYWOOD

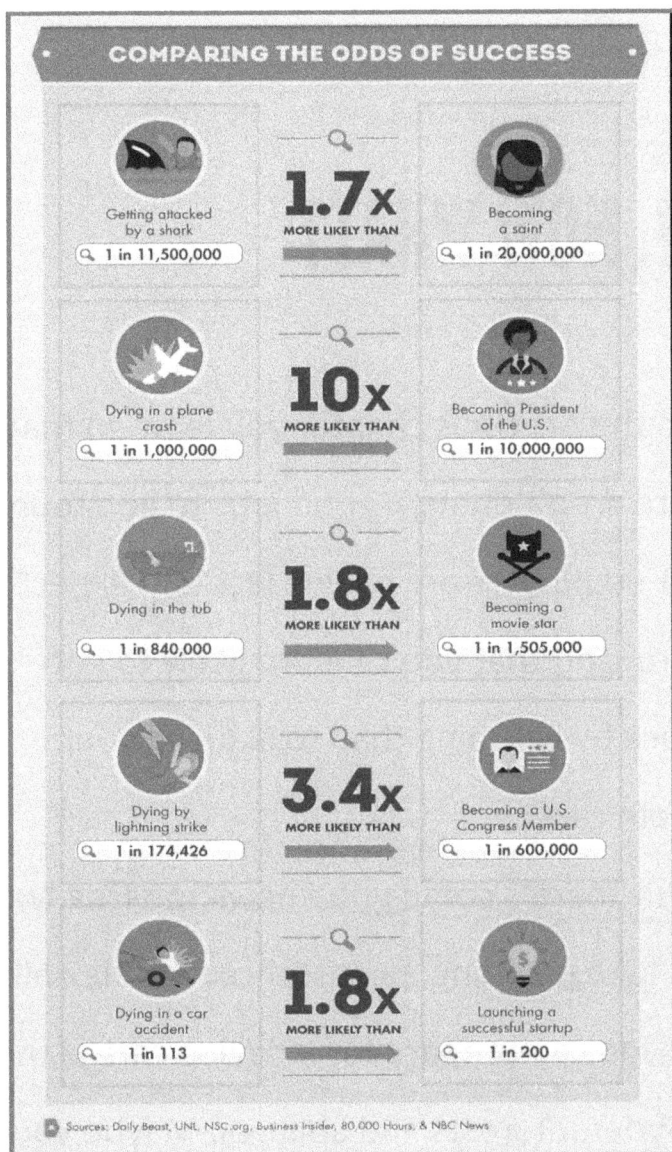

COMPARING THE ODDS OF SUCCESS

Getting attacked by a shark	**1.7x** MORE LIKELY THAN	Becoming a saint
1 in 11,500,000		1 in 20,000,000
Dying in a plane crash	**10x** MORE LIKELY THAN	Becoming President of the U.S.
1 in 1,000,000		1 in 10,000,000
Dying in the tub	**1.8x** MORE LIKELY THAN	Becoming a movie star
1 in 840,000		1 in 1,505,000
Dying by lightning strike	**3.4x** MORE LIKELY THAN	Becoming a U.S. Congress Member
1 in 174,426		1 in 600,000
Dying in a car accident	**1.8x** MORE LIKELY THAN	Launching a successful startup
1 in 113		1 in 200

Sources: Daily Beast, UNL, NSC.org, Business Insider, 80,000 Hours, & NBC News

Source: *https://www.onlinecasino.ca/odds-of-success*

2. NOW WHAT?

In the previous chapter you learned that there aren't enough good jobs to go around, that employers are paying less and expecting more, and that you're more likely to get struck by lightning than to achieve your dream career.

But there's some good news too (really). It will take planning, persistence, and flexibility, but you can prepare for a paying career that fits your interests and abilities. Maybe you can't be an astronaut, but if you follow these steps, you can launch your best career [38].

In the following pages you will get an overview of the **latest research** in organizations and careers, complete some useful **self-assessments**, and discover the array of employment and educational **opportunities** available to you.

WHAT ARE YOUR INTERESTS?

There is a tiny grain of truth in the advice to "follow your passion," and it is this: People whose work fits their interests and preferences tend to have happier and more successful careers [39]. It's risky to stake everything on your dream career. But it's smart to figure out in advance how much you enjoy (or can tolerate) working with your hands, interacting with people, manipulating numbers, or following a routine.

The **RIASEC** typology describes to what extent you would be comfortable in **R**ealistic, **I**nvestigative, **A**rtistic, **S**ocial, **E**nterprising, or **C**onventional jobs.

Realistic occupations are hands-on, practical, and often physical. Examples are forest ranger, auto mechanic, and quality control inspector.

Investigative occupations involve analyzing information and working in the realm of the theoretical. Investigative occupations include college professor, mathematician, and computer programmer.

Artistic occupations are intuitive and creative. This category contains dream jobs like photographer, illustrator, and musician. These are called "dream jobs" because if you think you can pay your bills with them, you're dreaming.

But Artistic types can make a decent living by helping other Artistic types pursue their dreams. For example, photographer Tony Northrup has a number of bestselling books on photography and photo enhancement software; musician Joseph Alexander has sold over 200,000 copies of his manuals on guitar technique; and one of mystery author Nancy J. Cohen's bestselling books is Writing the Cozy Mystery, an instructional book for aspiring mystery authors.

Social types are energized by working with people and helping them to solve their problems. Occupations in this category include counselor, social worker, and elementary school teacher. Social careers tend to be those that benefit society and help the young and the vulnerable, so they are not very well paid.

Enterprising occupations are those that involve managing, persuading, and making money. Sales, politics, and management careers fall into the enterprising category. These jobs tend to be well paid, and are suitable for thick-skinned extroverts.

Conventional careers are practical and predictable, and best suited to the conscientious and the patient. Conventional occupations include accountant, financial analyst, and IRS agent. If you think of yourself as a "big-picture" person who leaves the details to others, these jobs are not for you [40].

The O*Net Interest Profile, sponsored by the U.S. Department of Labor, measures your interests: **mynextmove.org/explore/ip**

Once you know your interests, you can search a database of careers:

onetonline.org/find/descriptor/browse/Interests

WHAT CAN YOU OFFER?

The RIASEC framework is focused on what you want from a job; the Skills Profiler tool is all about what you can offer an employer. This tool is useful for everyone, but it's especially important if you are starting out or changing careers. The profiler helps you translate skills you've developed into terms that employers understand and value. It also gives you an idea of what kinds of careers use those skills. The Skills Profiler is sponsored by the California Department of Education. Try it here: **cacareerzone.org/skills**

EMOTIONAL INTELLIGENCE

Emotional intelligence is the ability to know and manage your own feelings, and to sense and react appropriately to the feelings of others. It's a major predictor of workplace success [41-44], and can be as important as cognitive ability [45]. This isn't surprising, when you think about it. You need to be able to sense the mood of your manager, customer, or coworkers, and to respond appropriately. You should also be able to exercise self-control and avoid emotional outbursts in the workplace.

How emotionally intelligent are you?

One well-known measure of emotional intelligence is the Mind in the Eyes test. The MITE test requires you to read emotions based on a photo of a person's eyes.

You might think it would be impossible to read emotions from a black-and-white photograph of someone's eyes, but you may be surprised at how many items you get right. You can try the Mind in the Eyes for yourself at **socialintelligence.labinthewild.org/mite/**

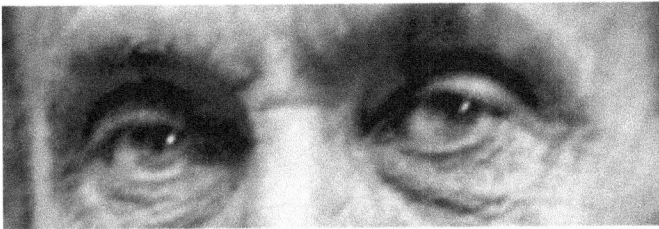

a. Playful   b. Comforting
c. Joking   d. Presidential
Not an actual item from the Mind in the Eyes test

Another test of the ability to discern others' thoughts is this verbal questionnaire that asks you to infer the motivations behind people's statements. You can take this test here: **openpsychometrics.org/tests/EI.php**

Can you increase your emotional intelligence?

It seems so. Emotional Intelligence appears to be related to physical brain function [46], but your brain is not unchangeable. Insufficient sleep, for example, can temporarily reduce your emotional intelligence [47]. And education and practice can help. Training managers in interpersonal and conflict resolution skills has been shown to lead to happier employees and higher productivity [48, 49].

How to improve your emotional intelligence

Executive coaching seems to work [50], but it can be expensive and time-consuming. Fortunately, there's a do-it-yourself solution. It will take a little effort, a lot of humility, and a few patient acquaintances.

This method depends on getting people's candid assessments of your interpersonal skills. This will be painful, but necessary.

We are very bad at judging our own interpersonal skills. Muriel Maignan Wilkins writes, "In my ten years as an executive coach, I have never had someone raise his hand and declare that he needs to work on his emotional intelligence. Yet I can't count the number of times I've heard from people that the one thing their colleague needs to work on is emotional intelligence. This is the problem: **those who most need to develop it are the ones who least realize it**." [51]

If you have accepted that your interpersonal skills might need some work, congratulations—you're already ahead!

Here's what to do next.

☐ Recruit friends, family members, teachers, and counselors to help you with this. Choose people who get along well with others.

☐ Promise them you will not get mad at them.

☐ Find a self-report measure of Emotional Intelligence. You can find some at: **eiconsortium.org/measures/measures. html** and **ihhp.com/free-eq-quiz**.

Or you can use the following five-item questionnaire [52]:

1. **Self-awareness** is the ability to observe yourself and recognize your feelings as they occur. How self-aware is_____?

2. **Managing emotions** means handling both negative and positive emotions well. How good is _____ at this?

3. **Self-motivation** includes controlling emotions to reach a goal, delaying gratification, and ignoring distractions. How self-motivated is _____?

4. **Empathy** is sensitivity to others' feelings and concerns, the willingness to see things from another's perspective, and acceptance of the differences in how people feel about and react to things. How empathetic is_____?

5. **Handling relationships** involves perceiving and managing emotions in others and displaying social competence and social skills. How is _____ at managing relationships?

☐ Distribute a paper copy or a link to the friends and family members who have agreed to help you and ask them to fill out the instrument on your behalf.

☐ Fill one out about yourself.

☐ Collect all the assessments. Thank everyone for their time and effort.

☐ Compare. Is your assessment of yourself very different from others' assessments? If four people who know you have rated you as not very perceptive of others' feelings, while you have rated yourself exceedingly high, you should consider the possibility that you're not as perceptive as you might believe.

☐ Remember your promise not to get mad at anyone. **Be appreciative, even if you are offended by the feedback**. Don't forget, you asked them to do this, and they took the time and effort to comply!

☐ Now you are armed with some knowledge and perspective. You have a good idea of **how others see you**, and where your self-image might be at odds with that. It's time to act.

☐ Practice **observing your own feelings** in a detached and unemotional way. This is something that people who are high in emotional intelligence do naturally. Their emotion and their self-reflection operate independently. They can step back and observe themselves.

☐ People with low emotional intelligence have their emotions all tangled up with their other mental processes [46]. Do your best to **"untangle"** when you think of it. For example, if you are feeling annoyed, ask yourself, why am I feeling this way? Does this barista/ cashier/ driver really deserve my wrath? Or am I angry because I experienced disappointment today, and this person crossed my path at the wrong time?

☐ Practice **taking responsibility** for your feelings and your behavior. Yes, there are people out there who are mean, or incompetent, or infuriating. And they can frustrate and upset you. Recognize and acknowledge those emotions. They are normal. But these feelings don't give you the right to make other people suffer. You don't have to yell, slam the door, or say things that will destroy relationships or careers.

☐ Practice **empathizing**. Try to imagine what it's like to be someone else, and observe the world through their eyes. The braggart, the know-it-all, or the undermine-y friend can be annoying. You may be tempted to put them in their place. But think about why they are acting this way. They may be insecure, so challenging their already-fragile self-esteem will only make things worse. Or they may be eager to share their knowledge, and unaware that they are dismissing other points of view. Is it really so important to set them straight?

☐ Accept that this is a **lifelong process**. The more you work on it, the more you'll **improve**.

PERSONALITY

There are many ways to measure aspects of your personality. These are a couple of the most popular and well-known.

The Myers-Briggs Type Indicator

The Myers-Briggs Type Indicator (MBTI) is very widely used. It's a proprietary test, which means that you have to pay for it and it can only be administered by a qualified professional. Fortunately, there are free tests online that will give you approximately the same results [53]. The Myers-Briggs Type Inventory is not meant to place people into jobs but is only intended to help people understand each other and work together and to aid in self-reflection. The MBTI measures these four preferences:

Extraversion vs. Introversion. Do you get your energy from being around people, or do you need alone time?

Intuition vs. Sensing. Do you think in abstract terms and see connections others don't, or do you feel more comfortable with the useful and the practical?

Thinking vs. Feeling. Do you make decisions based on facts and logic, or your feelings and values?

Judging vs. Perceiving. Do you prefer structure and schedules, or flexibility [54]?

Here are three sites that will give you MBTI-like results. Try them all and see whether they are consistent:

truity.com/test/type-finder-research-edition
similarminds.com/jung.html
humanmetrics.com/cgi-win/jtypes2.asp

The Big Five

Research has shown that personalities vary along five main dimensions. These are known as the Big Five or O.C.E.A.N. dimensions.

Openness to Experience covers intellect, imagination, and independence.

Conscientiousness is responsibility and dependability.

Extraversion characterizes someone who is talkative, assertive, and energetic.

Agreeableness describes someone who is trusting, good-natured, and cooperative.

Neuroticism is the opposite of calm and emotional stability.

Remember the RIASEC career interests? They line up with the Big Five personality dimensions as you might expect them to. Artistic and Investigative types are high in Openness. Enterprising types tend to be extroverted, while those with Social interests are both extroverted and agreeable [55].

The Big Five has never been as popular as the Myers-Briggs Type Inventory (MBTI), even though the Big Five has more research supporting its usefulness in the workplace [56, 57]. This may be partly because the MBTI was developed and commercialized by two dedicated individuals [58] while the Big Five / O.C.E.A.N. framework emerged from academic research. It may also be that the MBTI is popular with HR departments and corporate retreats because it won't hurt anyone's feelings. No matter which MBTI type you are, you can find something positive to say about it. Are you an ISTJ? According to the MBTI, you can be stubborn and insensitive, but you are also responsible and honest. An ENFP diagnosis marks you as emotional and impractical, but also charismatic and creative. Each type has its advantages and disadvantages, and its own place in an organization [59].

A Big Five assessment, on the other hand, might reveal you're unimaginative, neurotic, disagreeable, or lacking in conscientiousness. Who wants to hear that?

But even the Big Five characteristics have unexpected advantages and disadvantages, depending on one's situation and occupation. Openness to experience tends to be correlated with high academic achievement and verbal ability, so you might think that higher scores on this dimension are always better. But people with very high levels of openness to experience might not do well in jobs that require memorization or attention to detail [60].

Those high in neuroticism tend to be less

satisfied with their jobs and their lives than others. However, **neurotic or emotionally unstable people are more prevalent in creative occupations**, and this trait can be helpful in generating new ideas. Neuroticism combined with high conscientiousness is associated with better health [61, 62]. The tendency to worry appears to be associated with high workplace performance when combined with high intelligence [63].

Agreeableness helps you to work well in a team, but being *too* agreeable may work against a leader. Jobs that require you to disagree with or thwart others (labor negotiator, nightclub bouncer, police officer) require a certain level of disagreeableness.

Conscientiousness is a strong predictor of

workplace performance [64-66], but even this valued trait can have a downside. Conscientious people may not handle stress and setbacks as well as others. They experience lower well-being after unemployment [67] and may have a stronger fight-or-flight response in stressful situations [68].

If you want to take a Big Five test online and have it scored automatically, you can do it here:

openpsychometrics.org/tests/IPIP-BFFM/

Or you can take a quick paper test of your Big Five personality traits with the Ten Item Personality Inventory [69].

The Ten Item Personality Inventory

On a scale of 1 (disagree) to 7 (agree

strongly) write a number next to each statement to indicate the extent to which you agree or disagree with that statement. You should rate the extent to which the pair of traits applies to you, even if one characteristic applies more strongly than the other.

I SEE MYSELF AS

1. Extraverted, enthusiastic.   1 2 3 4 5 6 7

2. Critical, quarrelsome.   1 2 3 4 5 6 7

3. Dependable, self-disciplined.   1 2 3 4 5 6 7

4. Anxious, easily upset.   1 2 3 4 5 6 7

5. Open to new experiences, complex.   1 2 3 4 5 6 7

6. Reserved, quiet.   1 2 3 4 5 6 7

7. Sympathetic, warm.   1 2 3 4 5 6 7

8. Disorganized, careless.   1 2 3 4 5 6 7

9. Calm, emotionally stable.   1 2 3 4 5 6 7

10. Conventional, uncreative.   1 2 3 4 5 6 7

Scoring ("R" denotes reverse-scored items. To reverse-score, subtract the current score from 8. Seven becomes 1, 6 becomes 2, 5 becomes 3, 4 stays the same, 3 becomes 5, 2 becomes 6, and 1 becomes 7):

EXTRAVERSION: Take the average of 1 and 6R. The population average score is **3.98**

AGREEABLENESS: Take the average of 2R and 7. Average score is **4.91**

CONSCIENTIOUSNESS: Take the average of 3 and 8R. Average score is **4.94**

EMOTIONAL STABILITY: Take the average of 4R and 9. Average score is **4.56**

OPENNESS: Take the average of 5 and 10R. Average score is **5.46**.

You can find more information on how other test-takers scored, including sample size and standard deviation by age and gender, at **gosling.psy.utexas.edu**.

A newer variant on the O.C.E.A.N. model is the six-factor HEXACO, which adds Honesty-Humility as a sixth factor. You can take the HEXACO Personality Inventory at **hexaco.org/hexaco-online**.

RISK TOLERANCE

Are you willing to bet everything on getting your dream job, or would you rather work toward an attainable career goal? The Goal Motivation and Risk Tolerance Test will help you think this through. You can take it here:

psychologia.co/goal-motivation-and-risk-tolerance-test

HOW MUCH WILL YOU NEED TO EARN?

It can be eye-opening to discover how much you need to make to support the lifestyle you want. If you are happy living with a roommate in an inexpensive city with no children, few luxuries, and no vacations, you will have more career possibilities open to you.

Take this quiz to see what you need to earn to support your desired lifestyle.

jumpstart.org/what-we-do/support-financial-education/reality-check/

3. IS COLLEGE FOR YOU?

Should you go to college?

Should you go *now*?

It depends.

College graduates have higher salaries and lower unemployment rates than non-graduates. Graduates also enjoy better mental and physical health, better exercise habits, higher rates of voting and volunteering, and longer lives [70-72]. Policymakers and parents, seeing these numbers, have encouraged more and more high school graduates to go to college.

But as we saw earlier, the more college degrees are awarded, the less valuable they are in the labor market. **Pumping more college graduates into the economy doesn't magically make more jobs spring up to meet them**. A bachelor's degree does not guarantee a high income. As educational attainment has increased in the United States, so has the proportion of poor people with degrees [19, 20]. Around ten percent of the people living in poverty today in the United States have bachelor's degrees or higher, and around five percent of people with bachelor's degrees or higher live in poverty [19].

Simply comparing the outcomes of graduates and non-graduates doesn't reveal *why* college graduates have better job outcomes. Do universities simply select people who would make good employees and filter out those who wouldn't? Or would a given individual do better in life with a college degree than without one? It's impossible to run a truly randomized experiment in an ethical way. Two *unethical* ways you could answer this question would be to either (a) find a group of college-bound students and randomly bar half of them from higher education, or (b) take a group of non-degree-holders and randomly award half of them degrees from a reputable university.

It's unlikely that either of those studies will

be done, so researchers do their best to work around their limitations. They might compare students who are just above or below a cutoff point, or use detailed survey data to try to adjust for selection bias.

The studies that have been done suggest that **on average the college degree pays for itself** eventually, and on average **some college is better than no college** [32, 73, 74]. This is good news for a lot of people; fewer than sixty percent of full-time, first-time students complete their four-year degrees within six years [9].

MAJOR MATTERS

The areas of study that lead to the best-paid jobs are concentrated in engineering, computer science, business, and health care

[75, 76]. By contrast, the earning power of a completed arts or humanities degree is equivalent to not finishing college. The average man who goes to an expensive college for an arts degree won't see his additional earnings equal his college costs until age 54; the average woman with a fancy arts degree will never break even in her lifetime [32].

But **averages hide a lot of variation**, and don't take into account people's different motivations for attending college.

WHAT DO YOU WANT FROM COLLEGE?

If you want a lucrative career, keep in mind that **the best-paid occupations are those where you manage people, manage data, or manage money**. Attending a brand-name school is great if you have the opportunity, but remember that for undergraduate degrees, your **major is generally more important than your alma mater**. A business major from a top university will earn more than a business major from a non-selective university; but the business major from a non-selective university will earn more than an education major from a top university [77]. If you think business is boring and you want to follow your passion for early childhood education or counseling psychology, make sure you can afford it.

If you have your heart set on a particular school, don't be afraid to network. Spread the word that you are interested, and you might find that someone you know has a connection to your dream school. A good recommendation from a booster, faculty member or former student can make a difference.

WILL YOU GRADUATE?

To see the probability of someone with your characteristics graduating in 4, 5, and 6 years, see HERI's Graduation Rate Calculator, based on over 200,000 first-time, full-time college students: **heri.ucla.edu/GradRateCalculator.php.**

Your probability of completing college is higher if these apply to you [78]:

☐ You were reading by the 3rd grade

☐ You were absent less than 10% of the time in high school

☐ You failed no more than one class in ninth grade

☐ You took college classes in high school

☐ You did a summer bridge program

☐ You completed calculus in high school

Even for those who complete college, the lifetime returns to a four-year college degree can vary. Higher education is not exactly a great equalizer: those from low-income backgrounds have a return to a college degree of up to $500,000 (which is not too bad), while the college premium for graduates from high-income backgrounds is close to $1.4 million. The best-paying jobs accrue to those who are already more advantaged:

Individuals who earn a graduate degree,

are white or male, or come from a family with income above 400 percent of the poverty line, are much more likely to achieve very high earnings than similar individuals from a low-income family... whose earnings boost from college is particularly small. [79:27].

Is it ever not worth it to go to college? Personally, I believe that education has value in itself, and that the knowledge and critical thinking tools acquired in the course of a college education make life more meaningful and enjoyable. However, as far as financial return, college doesn't "pay off" for everyone. About a quarter of college graduates earn no more than those with a high school diploma [80].

WHAT IF YOUR CHANCES DON'T LOOK GOOD?

Let's say you've estimated that your chances of graduating from college are low, but you still want to go. What can you do to maximize your chances of getting through without drowning in debt?

If you want to avoid getting lost in the crowd, choose a school where undergraduate education is the top priority.

How can you tell whether undergraduate education is a priority?

Typically, an undergraduate-focused school will say their mission is based on **Liberal Arts** or a **Liberal Education**. These schools don't need to be expensive; check out the Council of Public Liberal Arts Colleges at **coplac.org**.

The term "liberal arts" refers to the traditional disciplines in a university: arts and sciences, as opposed to vocational education. A liberal arts –focused university has come to mean one that is mostly residential, emphasizes experimentation and intellectual growth, and represents undergraduate education at its best [81].

Research-oriented universities tend to be high-profile and highly selective. As their name implies, they are focused on producing research, not on teaching undergraduates. Visit **carnegieclassifications.iu.edu/lookup/lookup.php** and look up the university you're considering. If you see the classification *Doctoral Universities: Highest Research Activity,* you may want to eliminate that institution from your list for now. A research university is a great place to go for graduate school. But undergraduate education is not prioritized or rewarded at R1 institutions [82], and a struggling student is not likely to get a lot of support.

Once you've selected a few schools of interest, see whether you can talk to someone in Admissions. (If you can't get anyone to talk to you or call you back, cross the school off your list.) Ask what percentage of classes are fewer than 20 students (the best size for student success and persistence) and more than 50 (the worst) [83].

Ask what kinds of support programs you can join. Many schools have programs for first-generation, low-income, or other groups. Some schools offer summer bridge programs for the transition from high school to college; these are highly recommended.

STAY AWAY FROM FOR-PROFITS

Do not attend a for-profit institution. For-profits exist to funnel student loan money into their investors' pockets, and they are very good at that. Graduates of for-profits earn no more than high school graduates, and in some cases the relationship to earnings is negative [84]. Students who attend for-profits have more debt, higher rates of default, and worse job market outcomes compared to those who attend nonprofit schools [85].

To find not-for-profit institutions, you can

use the College Scorecard at

collegescorecard.ed.gov. Under "Advanced

Search," make sure *Private For-Profit* is

unchecked. You can also look up individual

institutions at **carnegieclassifications.iu.edu**.

4. ALTERNATIVES TO COLLEGE

If you decide to forego a college degree, you're not alone. Two-thirds of American adults don't have four-year degrees, and the high school diploma is still the most common entry-level credential [9].

CONSIDER A "DIRTY JOB"

Mike Rowe of "Dirty Jobs" fame has started a foundation to promote and support vocational arts education and the trades. He points out that while more and more high school graduates are heading to college, most jobs actually don't require a college degree: "We keep lending money we don't have to people who can't pay it back for jobs that don't exist." The website has an active jobs listing page at **jobs.mikeroweworks.org**. To find out more about the foundation, visit **mikeroweworks.org/about**.

EXPLORE OCCUPATIONS AT THE BUREAU OF LABOR STATISTICS

The Bureau of Labor Statistics is a great resource for information about careers. Let's say you want to search for occupations that pay well and don't require a college degree. Go to the Online Occupational Handbook at

bls.gov/ooh. On top of the page is a pulldown menu allowing you to select occupations by pay, education, and other factors. As of the current edition of this book, police detectives, criminal investigators, communication equipment workers, and logistics managers are among those occupations that typically earn over $75,000 annually and don't require a college degree.

SEARCH BY GEOGRAPHY

Once you have a job title you're interested in and you want to know whether there are any openings in a specific part of the United States, visit **careeronestop.org/Toolkit/Careers/Occupations/occupation-profile.aspx.** There you can type in a job title and zip code or state.

For example, a search for logistics managers in San Diego shows that the median salary is around $87,000 in San Diego and around $95,000 nationwide. (Note that that's the median salary for all people in this occupation, not the starting salary.) People starting in this career typically have a high school diploma or equivalent, although some current logistics managers have more or less schooling. From the *Outlook: Will there be jobs?* Window you can click the *Find job openings button* in the lower-left corner for live job listings.

CONSIDER A JOB THAT REQUIRES SOME ADDITIONAL EDUCATION

Some decent-paying jobs require training beyond high school, but not a four-year degree. Writing in U.S. News, Senior Editor for Personal Finance Susannah Snider and careers reporter Rebecca Koenig list the 25 highest-paying jobs that don't require a college degree from the U.S. News list of the 100 best jobs. Additional certification or training may be required [86].

U.S. NEWS TOP JOBS THAT DON'T REQUIRE A FOUR-YEAR DEGREE

Solar Photovoltaic Installer: $42,680

Auto Mechanic: $40,710

Insulation Contractor: $41,910

Massage Therapist: $41,420

Cement Mason: $43,000

Bus Driver: $42,080

Glazier: $43,550

Basic nursing care (LPN, LVN): $46,240

Carpenter: $46,590

Real Estate Agent: $48,690

Surgical Technologist: $47,300

Construction Equipment Operator: $46,990

Sheet Metal Worker: $48,460

Choreographer: $48,420

Insurance Sales Agent: $50,600

Brickmason / Blockmason: $50,950

Plumber: $53,910

Structural Iron and Steelworker: $52,770

Wind Turbine Technician: $54,370

Electrician: $55,190

Hearing Aid Specialist: $54,860

Sound Engineering Technician: $55,810

Sales Representative: $61,660

Executive Assistant: $57,410

Patrol Officer: $61,380

CONSIDER THE MILITARY

The military provides training, housing, and job placement benefits. Tuition Assistance is an educational benefit provided to active service members; each branch of the service has its own requirements. You can see each service's requirements and benefits at bit.ly/2E6MN0Z. In addition to tuition assistance, the Harry W. Colmery Veterans Educational Assistance Act, known as the GI Bill or the Forever GI Bill, provides educational benefits to those with 3 or more years of service. GI Bill benefits can be used for apprenticeship, vocational, bachelor's, and graduate education, and in some cases can be transferred to your spouse or children.

A military career is not for everyone. Success in the military requires physical and mental endurance, and a willingness to follow orders. When you enlist, don't just sign on the dotted line. Negotiate, read your enlistment contract carefully, and don't believe any promises that aren't written in the contract. Two thoughtful pieces to read before you make any life-changing decisions are

thebalance.com/what-the-recruiter-never-told-you-3332714

and

military.com/join-armed-forces.

You can find more detailed information about military benefits at **explore.va.gov**.

5. SO YOU'RE GOING TO COLLEGE

If you are planning to attend college, start preparing as early as you can. In high school, enroll in college prep or Advanced Placement courses and take as much math and writing as you can. This will keep your options open, no matter what you decide later. And start saving. Everyone talks about tuition costs, but books and living expenses can add up too. The following checklist starts in the first year of high school, but you don't have to start planning for college at age 14. Read over the suggestions and use whatever makes sense for you.

FRESHMAN YEAR

- ☐ Ask your guidance counselor or teachers what Advanced Placement courses are available, whether you are eligible, and how to enroll in them.

- ☐ Start your resume. Use it to keep a list of your awards, honors, paid and volunteer work, and extracurricular activities.

- ☐ Update your resume throughout high school. When you need to apply for jobs and scholarships, you don't need to hunt around for your information. You already have it in one file.

SOPHOMORE YEAR

- ☐ Meet with your school counselor or mentor to discuss colleges and their requirements.

- ☐ The two main qualifying tests for getting into college are the SAT and the ACT. Practice for the SAT by taking a practice Preliminary SAT/National Merit Scholarship Qualifying Test (PSAT/NMSQT) at **collegereadiness.collegeboard.org/psat-nmsqt-psat-10**. If you don't have internet access or a printer, try the public library. Tell the librarian that you want to take a practice test.

- ☐ For ACT practice, the Prepscholar site has a list of interactive and printable practice tests: **blog.prepscholar.com/complete-official-act-practice-tests-free-links**

☐ Make the best use of your summers: Work, volunteer, or take a summer course. You can enroll in noncredit courses, and sometimes even credit courses, at a nearby college or university.

☐ Plan to attend career and college fairs to talk to recruiters and get a more in-depth look at your options.

☐ Research majors that might be a good fit with your interests and goals based on your results from the U.S. Department of Labor's career search at **bls.gov/careeroutlook/.** But bear in mind that most people have no idea what they want to do when they're fifteen. Even those that do find themselves changing careers every few years once they're in the workplace.

☐ Keep taking math classes, and try to sequence your classes to complete calculus while you're in high school.

Successful completion of calculus is associated with success in college in general, and in science and technology specifically [87, 88].

JUNIOR YEAR

☐ Take the PSAT/NMSQT in the fall. You must take the test in 11th grade to qualify for scholarships and programs associated with the National Merit Scholarship Program. Check with your high school for the schedule.

☐ Register for and take the SAT and ACT for college admission. Your high school counselor should be able to tell you when and how to register. If your family is low income, or if you are an orphan, in foster care, or a ward of the state, you may qualify for a waiver.

☐ It's not too early to start looking for scholarship money! Use the Department of Labor's scholarship search at **careeronestop.org/toolkit/training/find-scholarships.aspx.** Some deadlines fall as early as the summer between 11th and 12th grades, so prepare now to submit applications soon.

SUMMER BETWEEN JUNIOR AND SENIOR YEAR: THE INFAMOUS FAFSA

You must fill out the FAFSA, or Free Application for Federal Student Aid, even if you don't think you qualify for federal student aid. Having filled it out is a prerequisite for scholarships, even those not based on financial need. Fill it out at **fafsa.ed.gov.** Note the **.gov** suffix, meaning that it's a website run by the Federal government.

On the FAFSA site you will create a

username and password called the *FSA ID*. You'll use your FSA ID to confirm your identity when accessing your financial aid information later. You must create your own FSA ID. If your parent creates it for you, that will cause confusion later and will slow down the financial aid application process.

DO NOT fill out FAFSA information at any site that doesn't end in .gov. These sites may charge you money or use your information for identity theft.

Need help? Go to the Federal Student Aid Information Center at **studentaidhelp.ed.gov/app/home/site/stud entaid**

SENIOR YEAR

Some institutions offer Early Admission or Early Decision. If you have competitive grades and test scores and you are sure that you would accept an offer from a specific institution without comparing offers, Early Decision is a good choice for you. If you want to compare different offers before you decide, Early Decision and Early Admission are probably not what you want to do.

Find out more at **professionals.collegeboard.org/guidance/applications/early**

Financial Aid: Grants, work-study, or loans?

Federal student aid comes in three flavors: Grants, work-study, and loans.

Grants are free money. Take them

whenever they're offered.

Work-study is where the Federal government subsidizes your employment on campus. This is a pretty good deal, as students with on-campus jobs usually have an easier time coordinating their work and school schedules and do better in school as a result.

Also, depending on what your work-study job is, you might have an opportunity to get to know your professors and/or staff members better and to make a positive impression on them. This can come in handy for building your network. You can draw on your contacts if you need career help or letters of recommendation later.

Student loans should be approached with caution. The Seattle Times reports that around 44 million Americans have student loan debt totaling $1.3 trillion. Unlike other loans, student loans are **nearly impossible to discharge in bankruptcy** [89]. While you may read about students graduating with hundreds of thousands of dollars in student loan debt, this is unusual. Most students who default have a relatively small balance. It's not necessarily bad to have a moderate amount of loan debt that you can afford to repay. What you want to avoid is defaulting on your loan. Students who attend for-profit institutions are about twice as likely to default [90]. Unsurprisingly, those with family wealth borrow less to begin with [91].

If you do take out a loan, plan to start paying off your loan the minute you graduate. **Even a single missed deadline can get you into trouble.** You can read more about types of student aid at **studentaid.ed.gov/sa/types.**

The Western Undergraduate Exchange

If you are a resident of one of the Western states, the **Western Undergraduate Exchange** program gives you discounted tuition in participating schools in the other WUE regions. See **wiche.edu/wue** for details.

WESTERN UNDERGRADUATE EXCHANGE

Alaska	Guam	Nevada	Utah
Arizona	Hawai'i	New Mexico	Washington
California	Idaho	North	Wyoming
Colorado	Montana	Oregon	Pacific Territories

The SAT and the ACT

The SAT and the ACT are two standardized tests commonly used in college admissions. Schools will generally accept either one. If you don't test well or wish to avoid standardized tests for other reasons, consider a "test optional" school. You can find a list of them here:

fairtest.org/university/optional

Ask your high school counselor whether your school provides free ACT and/or SAT testing.

If not, you can still take standardized tests for free if you are from a low-income household. You need to work with your high school counselor to arrange fee waivers.

Instructions for SAT fee waivers are here:

collegereadiness.collegeboard.org/sat/regist er/fees/fee-waivers

Instructions for ACT fee waivers are here: act.org/content/dam/act/unsecured/docum ents/FeeWaiver.pdf

Applying

Ask your counselor whether your high school provides financial aid for application fees. If not, **many universities will waive application fees** for financial need or good academic performance. You need to inquire with the schools individually to see what their policy is. **Be persistent**; many are reluctant to give up that $50 or $70 unless they must. Most universities will let you apply online.

The Common Application

The Common Application is a single application that lets you apply to over 700 institutions. It can save you a lot of time and effort, and it's free, although individual schools may still require their own application fee. You can find it at **commonapp.org**.

To apply, you'll need:

- [ ] A copy of your high school transcript

- [ ] A list of extracurricular activities, both school-related and non-school-related

- [ ] Test scores and dates from your college entrance exams (SATs, ACTs, SAT Subject Tests)

- [ ] PARENT / LEGAL GUARDIAN INFORMATION including educational background, occupational information, employer information, etc.

The Universal College Application, available at **universalcollegeapp.com**, is a smaller and shrinking competitor to the Common App. At one time it had close to 80 institutions, but now covers nine schools. The Coalition for College has 130 member schools and is available at **coalitionforcollegeaccess.org**.

Some schools are not in any common application consortium, so you will have to fill out separate applications for them.

Don't be afraid to apply to schools you think you can't afford. If you have documentable financial need, you may be able to get your application fee waived. Wealthy schools with large endowments can afford generous financial aid and may be more affordable than your state school.

Examine aid offers carefully to ensure they're offering you grants, not loans.

Schools that meet your financial need

These highly competitive schools will meet your entire financial need, without loans. See **blog.prepscholar.com/colleges-that-offer-complete-financial-aid** for updates.

SCHOOLS THAT MEET FINANCIAL NEED WITHOUT LOANS

Amherst	MIT	U. of Pennsylvania
Bowdoin	Northwestern	US Air Force Academy
Brown	Pomona College	US Naval Academy
Colby College	Princeton U.	Vanderbilt University
Columbia	Stanford U.	Washington and Lee
Davidson	Swarthmore	West Point
Harvard	U. of Chicago	Yale

Spring Semester of your senior year

- ☐ Visit colleges that have invited you to enroll, if you can afford the travel.

- ☐ Review your college acceptances and compare the colleges' financial aid offers.

- ☐ Contact a school's financial aid office if you have questions about the aid that school has offered you. In fact, getting to know your financial aid staff early is a good idea no matter what—they can tell you about deadlines, other aid for which you might wish to apply, and important paperwork you might need to submit.

- ☐ When you decide which school you want to attend, notify that school of your commitment and submit any required financial deposit. Many schools require this notification and deposit by May 1.

Do you need to go to a "top" school? It depends. If your goal is to work for an **elite investment bank, consultant, or law firm**, then you should plan to attend **Harvard or Yale** [92]. Otherwise, your alma mater is less important than your personal qualities and your major [93]. In fact, institution attended explains only a small amount of the variation in college graduates' earnings [94]. Life satisfaction after graduation is associated with the following experiences, no matter what kind of college you attended [95]:

- ☐ Engaging in meaningful jobs or internships
- ☐ Choosing courses requiring long-term work.
- ☐ Getting all the financial aid possible and available

☐ Working an on-campus job

☐ Keeping paid employment to under 20 hours a week.

☐ Keeping debt under $25K

IF YOU'VE BEEN OUT OF SCHOOL FOR A WHILE

☐ Consider a General Educational Development (GED) certificate if you don't have a high school diploma. Search online for "GED certificate" and your state's name.

☐ Research career possibilities using the Occupational Outlook Handbook at **bls.gov/ooh** and the career search tools at **mynextmove.org** and **careeronestop.org.** Your local community college may have career counselors willing to work with you.

- [ ] Use College Navigator at **nces.ed.gov/collegenavigator** to find the right school for you.

- [ ] Ask employers to recommend schools that provide training in the skills you will need for the career you choose.

- [ ] Ask your employer if assistance is available to help you pay for school.

- [ ] Use the U.S. Department of Labor's scholarship search at **careeronestop.org/toolkit/training/find-scholarships.aspx** to find scholarships.

- [ ] Apply for federal student aid by filling out the Free Application for Federal Student Aid. Find out more at **studentaid.ed.gov/sa/fafsa/filling-out.**

- [ ] Get to know the financial aid staff at the school you plan to attend; they can help you with aid applications and explain the types of aid available.

CHOOSING A MAJOR

Your own human capital—skills, work habits, ability to read others' emotions and control your own—will make a huge impact on your life and career. But when it comes to starting salary, major matters. Engineering, computer science, and finance majors make a lot of money; art, education and social work majors don't. You can see earnings by major from the National Center for Education Statistics at

nces.ed.gov/programs/coe/indicator_sbc.asp.
It's clear that if you want to make a good salary right out of college, pick something with "Engineering" in the title. But consider the unemployment rate as well, and decide what is most important to you. For example,

early childhood education majors have only 2.1% unemployment, but the average salary is low. You can find unemployment and **under**employment by major at **newyorkfed.org/research/college-labor-market/college-labor-market_compare-majors.html.** Above all, you should work in a job that you don't hate.

6. YOU'RE IN COLLEGE. DON'T MESS IT UP.

The transition from high school to college can be jarring, especially for students who didn't have to work that hard in high school. Suddenly most of your day is unstructured, and it seems you can spend most of your day goofing off without any negative consequences. You can't.

LEARN TO USE YOUR STUDY TIME

Watch Stephen Chew's video series, *How to Get the Most out of Studying*: **youtube.com/playlist?list=PL85708E6EA236E 3DB**. The six videos are between five and ten minutes each, and well worth your time. Among other things, you'll find that you're not necessarily the best judge of how much you're learning, that popular study methods like highlighting the textbook are not that effective, and that good old flashcards work really well.

ALWAYS SHOW UP FOR CLASS, EVEN IF IT'S NOT "REQUIRED"

Spending time in the classroom will not only help you to learn the material but can help you to make a good impression on the professor. Why would you care about that? Because you're not just after a passing grade. You need to start building relationships now that you can draw on later for job referrals and letters of recommendation.

DEVOTE AT LEAST TWO HOURS OUT OF CLASS STUDYING FOR EVERY HOUR YOU SPEND IN CLASS

This isn't some arbitrary rule professors made up to torture you. The credit hour is one hour of classroom or direct faculty instruction and a minimum of two hours of out of class student work each week for approximately fifteen weeks for one semester [96]. This is why 12 credits can be considered a full-time load. It's expected that in addition to the 12 hours you're spending in class, you're spending an additional 24 to 36 hours outside of class, studying and doing homework.

STAY INFORMED

Keep on top of relevant news in your industry and take every opportunity to enhance your general knowledge. Being well-informed will help you in the classroom and in the workplace, and will make your world a more interesting place to live in. Podcasts are a timesaver. You can listen while you are driving or doing chores. Some general-interest podcasts that are informative and not boring are *Planet Money*, *99% Invisible*, *The Constant*, *Make Me Smart*, *Stuff You Should Know*, and *Stuff You Missed in History Class*.

AVOID UNPAID INTERNSHIPS!

Only consider an unpaid internship if you are determined to work in a glamor industry like publishing, and the internship you are considering will give you amazing connections.

GET AN INTERNSHIP BEFORE YOUR SENIOR YEAR

Your part-time retail or work-study job is certainly work, and it might have aspects that look good on a resume. But the kind of job you are likely to have in college won't give you professional experience. This is where **internships** come in. (Internship-like experiences might also be called externships or co-ops.) Go to your school's internship or career office, if you have one.

CREATE A LINKEDIN ACCOUNT

If you don't have one already, create a LinkedIn account. Because you're still a student, it's appropriate to use your .edu email account. When you graduate and transition into the workforce, you will want to use an email account set aside for professional use.

Find keywords for your LinkedIn description.

Look for job and internship openings that interest you. Copy several of them and paste the text into a file. Open a word cloud generator like **tagcrowd.com** or **wordclouds.com**. Paste in the text from the ads you've collected and generate your word cloud. See if you can work the "big" words into your profile.

Make the most of your profile.

Make sure to fill out all the sections including Courses, Projects, Languages, Certifications, and Organizations.

Connect

Start building your network while you're still in college. Use LinkedIn to connect with your professors, classmates, and acquaintances. Because LinkedIn is a professional network, not a social one, people will tend to react positively to a connection request. Explore LinkedIn's Company pages **linkedin.com/company** and resources for students at

university.linkedin.com/linkedin-for-students.

DON'T DO ANYTHING ~~STUPID~~ ON SOCIAL MEDIA

It's safest to avoid social media entirely, but that may not be realistic. In any case, don't post, email, or write anything you wouldn't want the world to see. Avoid politics (not all employers will share your views). Don't post pictures of yourself in costume. A topical costume may seem funny at the time, but may not age well.

Sexy Ebola Containment Suit

Item Details

As the deadly Ebola virus trickles its way through the United States, fighting its disease is no reason to compromise style. The short dress and chic gas mask will be the talk of Milan, London, Paris, and New York as the world's fashionistas seek global solutions to

Not recommended for the company party

Don't post anything about drug use or drinking. Drinking alcohol is perfectly legal if you are of age, but that didn't stop a teacher from losing her job over a private Facebook photo [97].

This is one of the vacation photos that got schoolteacher Ashley Payne fired to "voluntarily" resign from Apalachee HS in Georgia. She sued, and lost.

TWITTER CAUTION

Twitter makes it easy—maybe too easy—to post your thoughts. Tweeting before thinking can be a career-killer [98]. Even if all your tweets are perfectly proper, marketers (with the help of IBM) can infer your personality traits from your Twitter profile. See what others can see at **personality-insights-demo.ng.bluemix.net/**

Let's look at some real tweets by college students and see what we can learn.

WHAT'S WRONG WITH THIS TWEET?

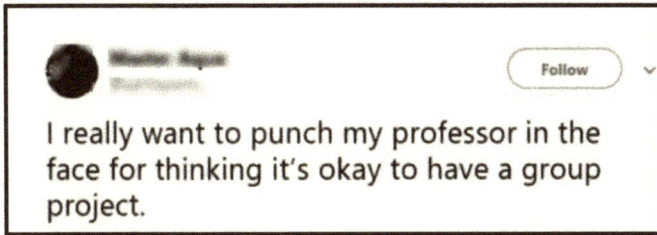

I really want to punch my professor in the face for thinking it's okay to have a group project.

Employers value teamwork; avoiding group projects gives the impression you don't work well with others.

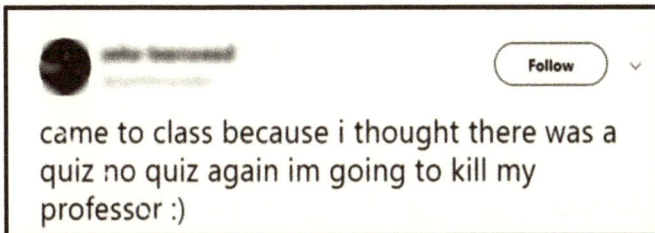

came to class because i thought there was a quiz no quiz again im going to kill my professor :)

Organizational skills are key. If you are prone to scheduling mix-ups, don't announce it to the world.

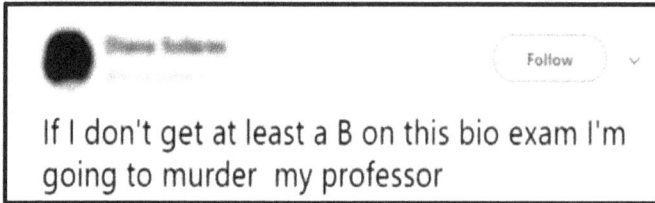

If I don't get at least a B on this bio exam I'm going to murder my professor

High standards are great, but so is taking responsibility for one's own academic performance.

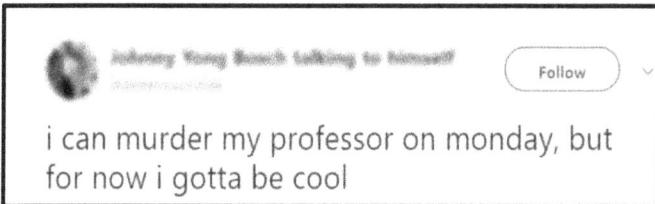

i can murder my professor on monday, but for now i gotta be cool

And don't announce your intention to injure or murder your professor. This can get you a visit from the FBI [99]. (On the bright side, you won't have to worry about your job search for a few years).

7. GET READY TO FIND A JOB

If you did an internship and it worked out well, you might have a job offer in hand before you graduate. Congratulations! And be careful. Some companies will withdraw your offer if they find out you're looking for another job. Find out if this is the case. If you're allowed to shop around, do. You'll be in a strong negotiating position as you already have an offer in hand.

If you don't have a job lined up **by the start**

of your senior year, you might have trouble finding something. The summer before your final year of college is the time to secure your first job.

YOUR SOCIAL NETWORK (THE REAL-LIFE KIND)

No later than the beginning of your senior year, go to the professors you really clicked with, and ask them if they would be **willing to be a reference** for you. Do the same with staff members and anyone you worked for. At this point you don't need to ask them to write recommendation letters. Keep their names and email addresses on hand, ready to provide as references should anyone ask. Be prepared to take "no" for an answer. It's better to have someone honestly decline than to provide you a weak or negative reference.

As you revisit your social network, people may try to give you advice. Listen and thank them. Their intentions are probably good, and they most likely just want to help.

If the advice turns out not to be useful, then don't use it. But make a note of it, and keep an open mind.

YOUR ELEVATOR PITCH

An elevator pitch is a thirty-second version of your story. The idea is that if you find yourself in an elevator with your ideal employer, you can introduce yourself and make a good impression in the short time you have together. Professional services firm PwC suggests composing your elevator pitch in three parts:

Who are you? "Hello, my name is Penny Priddy. I'm a senior at Fugue State University, majoring in aeronautical engineering with a minor in music history."

What are your unique accomplishments, interests, and skills? "I interned last summer at Yoyodyne Propulsion Systems, where I worked on the design of the YP-100 oscillation overthruster and developed a passion for interdimensional teambuilding."

What do you want? "I saw that your company is expanding its interdimensional research efforts, which is why I came this conference. I'm very interested in the mission of the Banzai Institute, and I would like to work for the Banzai Institute's Research and Development Division."

For more, see PwC's worksheet at

https://www.pwc.com/c1/en/assets/downl oads/personal_brand_workbook.pdf

YOUR ONLINE PRESENCE

Your future employers (as well as employees, coworkers, romantic prospects, and acquaintances) will search for you online. Because you paid attention to the previous chapter, your social media profile is blameless and squeaky-clean. Good job!

But just to be on the safe side, set up a Google alert on your name. That way, you'll see when something gets posted about you. If you have a very common name, you might want to skip this to avoid getting inundated with irrelevant email alerts.

Go to Google Alerts at **google.com/alerts**. At the top of the page is a box with a magnifying glass icon. Enter your name and select the "Create Alert" button that appears.

Then select how often you want to get alerts (once a week is probably enough) and other options. Once you set this up, you'll get an email when your name is mentioned online.

YOUR EMAIL ADDRESS

Set up a separate, professional-sounding email address for the sole purpose of career activities. Do not use it for social, leisure, or family communication. You will use this professional email address to sign up for LinkedIn and other job-related services and to communicate with employers and recruiters.

A Gmail address is generally considered to be more work-appropriate than Yahoo, AOL, or Hotmail, which are best used for personal communication. Before you sign up, set up a free Gmail account that is exclusively for job-related things. Using the name Patience Fairweather as an example, the format **patience.fairweather [at] gmail.com** or **p.fairweather [at] gmail.com** will work.

Mail.com offers free email accounts with a selection of domains. If one of the available domains suits your career aspirations, you may want to get an address like **p.fairweather@consultant.com** or **patience@therapist.net**.

If you want your email address customized, as in **patience@fairweather.com**, you'll need a custom domain. For this you will need to purchase a domain name at a site like **namecheap.com** and follow the instructions there to set up your email account.

FUN SOCIAL MEDIA: FACEBOOK, TWITTER, INSTAGRAM, SNAPCHAT, ETC.

If you have social media accounts, make sure to keep your personal and professional separate, and to have strong privacy settings on your personal accounts. Facebook knows a lot about you, including things you never meant to tell it [100]. Detailed instructions for adjusting Facebook privacy settings are at **facebook.com/help/325807937506242**.

If you leave town for an interview or any other reason, don't post anything about travel plans until after you return from your trip. You don't want to lay out the welcome mat for burglars, and you don't want potential employers to think you're naïve about security.

SERIOUS SOCIAL MEDIA: LINKEDIN

If you're looking for a job, **you need a LinkedIn profile**. It may be the first thing that comes up when someone searches for you online, so it has to look good. A strong profile can help you build your resume, keep connected with your alumni network, and maintain an online presence that will enhance your job search.

If you don't already have a LinkedIn profile, it's straightforward to set one up. Go to **linkedin.com**. If you're not logged in, you'll be invited to join the site.

Setting up your account will take some time and thought. You'll be asked to enter information about your education, work experience, publications, and skills.

NO, YOU CAN'T BE AN ASTRONAUT

YOUR GENERAL RESUME

Once you've completed your LinkedIn page, you'll have a head start on your resume. Some companies will let you apply to jobs using your LinkedIn account as your resume. This can save you a lot of time, but those employers are the exception.

Most employers still require a separate application and a resume tailored to the specific position. Still, having a standard resume to work from can be a big help.

It's not necessary to bother with fancy formatting, as most resumes are now machine scanned by an Applicant Tracking System (ATS). Your application has a better chance if your resume is easy to scan.

MACHINE-READABLE RESUME OUTLINE:

FIRSTNAME LASTNAME

Mailing Address
Phone number you can answer anytime
A professional email address

OBJECTIVE or SUMMARY

You can pull from a summary from your elevator pitch

KEYWORDS

Optional; for important keywords that don't seem to fit anywhere else

EDUCATION

Most recent first
If you are a new graduate, put any honors like the Dean's List here

EXPERIENCE

Put job-relevant experience here. For each position, list an accomplishment. For example, increased daily page visits from 10 to 100

OTHER EXPERIENCE

Optional. Semesters abroad, unrelated internships and honors

ACTIVITIES

Optional. Clubs, sports, volunteer work

SKILLS and CERTIFICATIONS

This section is very important. Put certifications and specific software skills here

TIPS FOR MACHINE-READABLE RESUMES:

- ☐ Executive resume writer Lisa Rangel suggests putting your name and the desired position as the title: "Your Name – Marketing Director."

- ☐ Be specific when describing your past positions and accomplishments. Use employer names; omitting them can seem like you're hiding something.

Include any achievement that can be described in numbers like "Increased revenues by 30%."

- [ ] Adecco's Jenni Chelenyak recommends using a separate line for each element of your contact information and ending company names with terms like LLC, Inc., Co., and Corp. This helps the software recognize the companies and put them in the right category.

- [ ] Use Arial, Helvetica, or Times Roman in 10 or 12-point font. These are considered standard and most scanners will be able to handle them.

- [ ] Use recognizable words in the headings: Objective / Summary, Experience, Employment, Work History, Positions Held, Appointments, Skills, Summary,

Summary of Qualifications, Accomplishments, Strengths, Education, Affiliations, Professional Affiliations, Publications, Papers, Licenses, Certifications, Examinations, Honors, Personal.

☐ Do not combine two headings into one. Avoid rare or unusual words.

☐ An **Objectives** section is appropriate for a new job seeker; a **Career Summary** is appropriate for someone with substantial work experience.

☐ Use Rich Text Format (RTF) for your resume unless the application instructions tell you otherwise. Test your resume's readability by copying and pasting

it into a simple text editor like
WordPad.

☐ Don't use underlining or other
formatting.

☐ Scan your resume to see what the
machine sees at **jobscan.co**.

☐ If you don't mind signing up for a
mailing list, submit your resume
to **topresume.com/resume-
review** for a free critique.

☐ For more on crafting your
resume, go to Purdue's Online
Writing Lab:
**owl.purdue.edu/engagement/jo
b_search_resources/resumes/ind
ex.html**

If you have a friend or relative who works

in Human Resources, manages employees, or

reads a lot of resumes, have them look over

yours. You don't have to take every

suggestion they give you, but listen to their feedback. You are likely to learn something useful.

8. GET A JOB

Whether you're still in school or switching jobs or careers, be prepared to spend a lot of time and effort on finding a job. Treat your job search like a job in itself—a job with no boss to guide you, no coworkers to commiserate with, and no HR department to complain to. You'll need to be persistent, organized, and thick-skinned.

KEEP TRACK OF YOUR SEARCH

Technology has made it easy to apply for

jobs. Instead of printing out resumes and cover letters on fancy paper and paying for postage, you can apply for jobs entirely online. But this means that the companies you want to work for are likely getting hundreds of applications for each open position.

In addition, many posted jobs don't really exist. Some job "interviews" are really an attempt to get industry or competitor information; some jobs are not quite as advertised, for example commission-only instead of salaried; some positions are going to an inside applicant, but the rules require a national search. This means you should plan on sending out hundreds of applications. An app called JibberJobber (**JibberJobber.com**) can help you keep track of your search. It's free for up to 25 contacts, so you can use it and decide whether you like it before paying for a subscription.

You can also create your own spreadsheet. Columns to include are:

Company Name	The name of the organization
First Contact	Your initial point of contact at the company.
App Contact	Who you addressed your cover letter to. Sometimes the name is not available, so just put the title or committee name.
Source	Where you saw the ad posted or who told you about the position.
Date Applied	When you submitted your application.
Application Summary	What you submitted: a cover letter, resume, and any additional materials

Response	Who got back to you, when, what they said.
Interview	When and where your interview is/was scheduled, interview notes afterward.
Follow-Up	What you sent (thank you email or letter) and when.
Date of last contact	Sort your sheet by date of last contact to follow up if you haven't heard from them in a while.

Every time you send out an application or get a response, make a note of it. Make sure your spreadsheet is somewhere you can access. Use a service like Dropbox or Google Drive and back it up regularly. Make sure you can access it using your phone.

If you happen to be away from your desk when you get a call, you'll want to the information available to you.

SET UP DAILY EMAIL ALERTS

If your college or university has an active career office, sign up for any services they offer. Whether you are working with a career services office or not, make sure you have job announcements coming into your mailbox every day.

LinkedIn

SETTING UP A JOB ALERT ON LINKEDIN:

☐ Search for a job on LinkedIn.

☐ At the top of the left panel of the job search results page, switch the Job alert toggle to **On** to create a job alert for your current search criteria.

☐ Or set-up a job alert by switching the Create alert for this search toggle button at the bottom left of the search results page to **On**.

- [ ] In the Create search alert pop-up, select how often you'd like to receive alerts about new jobs on LinkedIn.com that fit those specific search parameters from the Receive alert dropdown. The available options are daily or weekly.

- [ ] Select how you'd like to get notified from the Get notified via dropdown. The available options are email, notifications, and email & notifications.

- [ ] Click Save.

USAJobs (U.S. citizens and legal residents)

SETTING UP A JOB ALERT ON USAJOBS

- [ ] Sign into USAJOBS. If you don't have a profile, you need to create one. Only signed in users can save their search.

- ☐ Start a job search by entering a keyword or location in the search box and click Search.

- ☐ Narrow your results using filters.

- ☐ Click Save this search on the search results page located above the search results.

- ☐ Name your search—this will help you manage your saved searches.

- ☐ Choose how often you want to get notified. We recommend daily if you're looking for very specific jobs, since some jobs can open and close within a week.

- ☐ Click Save.

Other job search sites

- ☐ **CareerBuilder.com**

- ☐ **RobertHalf.com**

- [ ] **Indeed.com**

- [ ] **Glassdoor.com**

- [ ] **Ziprecruiter.com/search-jobs**

- [ ] **Monster.com**

Specialized Sites

- [ ] Accounting and finance: **cpajobfinder.com/jobs, efinancialcareers.com**

- [ ] Culinary and restaurant: **culintro.com**

- [ ] Healthcare: **healthcarejobsite.com, healthcareadministrationjobs.net**

- [ ] Higher education: **higheredjobs.com, insidehighered.com, chronicle.com.**

- [ ] Programming and tech: **Dice.com, TechCareers.com, Stackoverflow.com Crunchboard.com.**

YOUR DAILY SCHEDULE

If you are still in school, or currently employed, you'll only be able to use this schedule on weekends and holidays and will have to do what you can in your free hours during the week.

If you are currently between jobs, you should plan to follow this schedule just as you would a regular job. It may help to take your laptop to a library or coffee shop, just to get out of the house and feel like you're at work.

When is your brain at its best?

You need to figure out what time of day you're most productive. Once you know your best brain time, set aside those two hours or so for writing cover letters and customizing your resume. Use the less-productive hours for more routine tasks like sending out completed applications, filling in your tracking information, and finding new jobs to apply for.

Many people find they can **concentrate for 20 minutes at a time**, after which they start to lose focus. This varies among individuals, of course, but it's a general enough rule that there is a popular time-management method, called the **Pomodoro Method**, that involves working in 20-minute bursts with 5-minute breaks in between. (The method's inventor originally used an Italian kitchen timer shaped like a tomato—*pomodoro* is Italian for tomato—to time his work.) You can use this method to work through your most productive two hours.

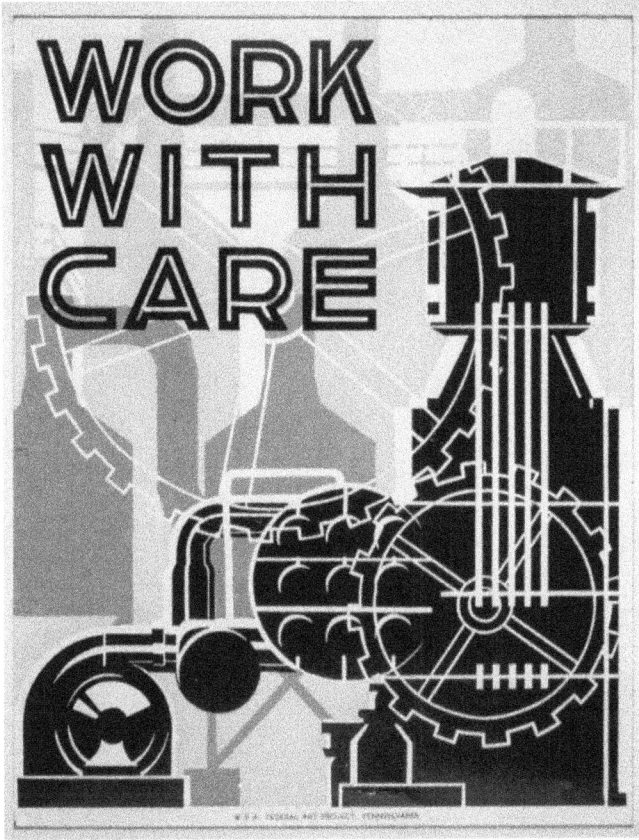

How do you know when your brain is at its best? Observe yourself for a few days and see when you are most able to tackle challenging tasks like writing or starting a project. Or you can take the online questionnaire at

cet-surveys.com/index.php?sid=61524

SAMPLE WEEKDAY SCHEDULE for
SOMEONE WHOSE PEAK TIME is 10 to NOON

7am:

Wake up, have a cup of coffee, take a half-hour walk, and come back and shower. This will start you off with mild exercise and sunlight, good for your cognition and mental health.

8-10am:

Because your brain's not fully up and running, do moderately-taxing tasks. Open your job search email account and go through the day's jobs. Save the ones you intend to apply for, and record them on your spreadsheet. Delete the ones you don't intend to apply for.

Fix yourself breakfast.

Read some industry news.

Set up for your productive time:

Find the announcements for the jobs you
are going to apply to, and similar jobs that
may not be in your desired location.

Copy similar jobs into a single document.

Then copy and paste the text into a word
cloud generator such as **tagcrowd.com** or
wordclouds.com. In
this word cloud
for hotel
manager
positions,
unexpected words
include "experience," "vision," "financial,"
and "team." You now have general keywords

for your cover letter. You might emphasize that you are fluent in the **financial** as well as the people aspects of the job, and that you can direct your **team** to translate your employer's **vision** into a consistent **guest experience**.

10am-noon:

This is your productive time. You will customize your resume and write a cover letter for each position.

Customizing your resume and cover letter

- ☐ Open up the word cloud generator again.
- ☐ Copy and paste in the text from the particular job you're applying to.
- ☐ Open a new window. Go to the company website and find the Mission

Statement, the Vision Statement, and/or the "About Us" description. Paste these into the same word cloud box.

☐ Generate your company-specific word cloud.

☐ These keywords reflect the company's aspirations for itself. Work them in wherever they fit. You can even put them into the "keywords" section of your resume if appropriate.

☐ Some applications require a cover letter, while others make it optional. Always submit a cover letter if you can.

☐ In your cover letter, strike a tone that is confident but not overconfident. Flatter the employer ("It is with great pleasure that I am seeking an employment opportunity with your institution. It is a well-respected company and I would be proud to be a part of it.") [101]

☐ Before you submit your resume and cover letter, run a spell check. Then run the documents through a machine scan simulator like **jobscan.co**. What comes out of the machine scan should look like what's described in the job announcement.

☐ If the scan results don't look right, edit your resume and try again.

- [ ] Proofread everything before sending. A single typo can disqualify you.

- [ ] Focus on sending a few well-crafted applications to jobs that are a good match. Don't just blast out a generic resume to any position that's remotely a fit.

- [ ] As soon as you complete each application, record the relevant information into JibberJobber.com or your spreadsheet.

12pm-2pm:

Break for lunch. Turn off the computer. Go for a walk. Exercise. Do your grocery shopping. Get the laundry done. If you haven't showered or brushed your teeth yet, do it now.

2pm until bedtime:

Allocate your time among people-oriented activities like volunteering and networking, and solitary ones like reading industry news and relevant blogs. Alison Green, the woman behind the wonderful *Ask a Manager* blog (bookmark it now at **askamanager.org**) recommends boosting your job search by **volunteering**, **reconnecting**, and **networking**:

Volunteering.

Volunteering has three advantages: First, volunteering **helps other people**. Second, volunteering can help you to **build your network** and get connected to job opportunities. Finally, volunteering can **help you to avoid a gap in your resume**. A mainstream organization such as the Red

Cross or United Way will be appealing to most employers. A church-related organization might not carry as much weight with employers, as they may assume your service is simply part of your church membership. If you can get onto the board of a nonprofit, that's ideal, but director positions are competitive. Any computer, bookkeeping, or marketing skills that you can contribute are likely to be useful and in high demand.

Reconnecting.

Invite your former co-workers, old bosses, and friends to lunch or coffee. Don't pressure them to provide you with job leads. Instead, use the time to catch up.

Reconnecting expands your network and

the possibility of hearing about a position. It's also good for your mental health, as it helps you to avoid becoming too isolated.

If you are an introvert, try to force yourself to do this at least once a month.

Networking.

Join professional organizations in your field. Your local Chamber of Commerce or Junior Chamber of Commerce are a good start. Service clubs like Rotary, Kiwanis, or Lion's Club are a great way to meet local employers and benefit your community. Industry-specific associations can be helpful both for making contacts and keeping your knowledge current.

You might have the opportunity to take on a leadership position in one of these groups.

If you can commit to doing the work well, do it. This will look great on your resume and will help you to build your network and generate goodwill.

YOUR PRE-INTERVIEW CHECKLIST

Congratulations, you've been invited to interview! Whether it's on the phone, via video, or in person, you need to prepare thoroughly beforehand.

Don't be like the young lady who, when interviewing with IBM, volunteered that she admired their "Xerox machines." Or the gentleman who, when asked why he had chosen to interview with a specific company during on-campus interviews, replied, "Because you guys were on the list." Neither one got the job.

Research the company:

☐ Find the company's mission statement and vision statement. Strictly speaking, the vision is where the company wants to be in the future ("A Yoyodyne personal interdimensional overthruster in every American household") while the mission is what the company does every day ("Yoyodyne is a vertically-integrated company that bakes quality into every part of the manufacturing process"). Some companies have only a mission statement or a vision statement, while others have both. Some have neither and opt instead for "about" or "who we are." You should be able to show your interviewer that you are familiar with the company's self-image and aspirations.

☐ Research the company's **financial health,** including any big decisions or events that might affect its future. Is the company publicly traded? That is, do they sell stocks on a stock exchange like NASDAQ? If so, they'll have an Investor Information page. That will provide information about the financial health of the company. **Bloomberg.com**, **Yahoo Finance**, and other free sites can also be a good source of company information.

☐ Whether the company is publicly traded or not, do an online search for news of the company. If the company is small, you might find something in the online archives of the local newspaper.

☐ See where the company operates. **Are they local, nationwide, or international?** Do they have international customers or partners, and if so, are you willing to travel internationally? If you don't have a current passport, be prepared to tell the interviewer that you are in the process of getting one. If you are a U.S. citizen, apply for a U.S. passport at **usa.gov/passport.**

☐ Find out where the department fits within the company. How does it work with or overlap other departments, and are there possible interdepartmental rivalries?

☐ Figure out the company's **business model**, or how it makes its money. For example, social media companies and search engines get their revenue not from the people who use their services, but from advertisers who want to reach those people. Printer companies don't make their money from selling printers; in fact, they often lose money on the printer itself but make it up by selling expensive printer cartridges.

Check LinkedIn

- [ ] Find out whether anyone you know works at that company or has a connection there. If you are comfortable contacting this person, reach out, share your good news (you are very excited about your upcoming interview with Yoyodyne's new Consumer Devices Division) and ask for any advice or tips your contact might have. People are generally happy to be asked for advice.

- [ ] If you know the name of the person who will be interviewing you, you might want to look them up. But be aware that LinkedIn can tell them that you viewed their profile.

Find out about salaries and interview

experiences at Glassdoor

☐ Read the company's reviews at
glassdoor.com/Reviews/index.htm,
but keep an open mind. Anyone can
post there.

☐ Look at the salary information, but
again, keep in mind that it may not be
entirely accurate:
glassdoor.com/Salaries/index.htm

Prepare yourself

☐ If you have an **in-person interview**,
make sure you know how to get there.
Take a drive out to the building. Time
how long it takes and make a note of
where you can park.

☐ If you have a **video interview**, test your
setup beforehand and make sure the
background is clean and professional. A
blank wall or a bookshelf (stocked with
non-controversial books) is best. A

window looking out on a view may be tempting, but you never know whether something distracting might happen outside. You don't want to be upstaged by weather or wildlife.

- [ ] If you have an in-person interview scheduled, make copies of your resume and other important documents (cover letter, list of references, etc.) in advance. Don't expect that your interviewers will have read or remembered your resume.

- [ ] If you have a phone or video interview, have a paper copy of your resume close by. You don't want to blank if you're asked about specific details or dates.

- [ ] Do your best to memorize your elevator pitch but have a printout handy too. This is what you'll use to answer the "tell me about yourself" question.

☐ Prepare to be asked, ***"Why are you leaving your current job?"*** This doesn't apply if you're interviewing straight out of school, but if you are leaving another job, the right answer is something like "I'm happy where I am, but I'm looking for the opportunity to develop XYZ skill and/or work with XYZ technology." Never, never badmouth your employer or coworkers.

☐ Prepare to answer the question, ***"Why do you want to work for us?"*** This is the corporate equivalent of "tell me you love me." Pick something the company is likely to be proud of. "Yoyodyne products are the best in the industry and I'd be honored to work with the world-class engineers in the Consumer Devices Division."

☐ Prepare an answer to the question, *"What's your greatest weakness?"* Sorry, you can't say you work too hard.

What's your greatest weakness?

To respond to this question, pick something **that isn't too bad**, and importantly, make sure it's something **you have found a way to fix**. "I'm an introvert, so in my previous sales job that involved ten straight hours of cold-calling, I found that I was getting a little worn-out toward the end of the day."

Next, talk about **how you're working on it**: "I've been very deliberate about getting sufficient sleep, exercising regularly, and packing an energy bar when I have a day of dealing with people ahead of me. I've found that this way I can put in twelve-hour workdays with no drop in energy, and last month I was the most productive salesperson on my team."

Your answers should take the company culture into account. If you know that the company has a hard-driving culture where people brag about having no work-life balance and never getting more than four hours of sleep, you need to take that into consideration. Some interviewers want to hear "I make sure to take care of myself and get enough sleep," while others would prefer "I'm successfully training myself to be more and more productive."

Prepare to be asked whether you have any questions of your own.

The worst response is probably something

like, "so you guys don't do background checks or anything, right?" But the second-worst response is, "no, I don't have any questions." Consultant Rachel Weingarten recommends asking your interviewer questions like these:

- [ ] ***Why did you join the company?*** Does the interviewer seem genuinely happy about the job and the company? If they can't think of anything nice to say, that may be a red flag.

- [ ] ***How does this role further your company's mission?*** This will give you an idea of where the job you're interviewing for fits into the big picture, and whether its occupant is likely to have built-in enemies.

- [ ] ***Tell me about your most successful employees***. What do they do differently? The answer will tell you a lot about what the company values.

☐ *What do you expect someone in this position to accomplish in the first 60-90 days?* It's good to know what their expectations are.

☐ *What, if anything, in my background gives you pause?* The answer may give you a chance to address concerns, in the interview and/or in your thank-you note.

☐ *What is the turnover in the department I'm interviewing for?* This is a tricky one; if you sense this question may make them defensive, don't ask it. But higher than average turnover for the industry might be a red flag.

☐ *What are the opportunities for growth and advancement?* This is good to know, and assures your interviewer that you're looking at staying for the long term.

☐ *If you had a chance to interview for your company again, knowing what you know now, what questions would you ask next time?* The answer can be very informative. Your interviewer might even enjoy sharing some insight.

☐ *What haven't I asked that most candidates ask?* Your interviewer may not know how to answer this one. But if you do get an answer, it's probably going to be a pretty useful one.

☐ *What are the next steps in this process?* This is a graceful way to end your questions, and you want to know the answer anyway.

Once you have prepared answers and questions, *conduct at least one practice interview,* and ideally run through it two or three times. Your college career center might be able to set up a practice interview for you, but if not, a friend, family member, or roommate can do it. Don't skip this step. **Tell your "interviewer" to be tough on you**. Have them ask a few "illegal" questions about your age, family, marital status, or ethnic background. Practice now and you're less likely to choke when it happens for real.

The day before the interview

- [ ] Make sure you have stamps, nice notecards, and a decent pen. **You will be writing a thank-you note**, and a handwritten note is usually preferable. A set of simple, cream-colored thank-you cards, and a blue or black gel pen are good choices.

- [ ] Only when you've prepared all your answers and questions should you think about **what to wear**. Don't spend hours picking out your interview ensemble and procrastinating on everything else.

☐ You want your interviewers to remember you, not your outfit. Check the company's website to see how the managers dress. If you're not sure of the company's dress code, err on the side of caution. When in doubt, cover tattoos, knees, elbows, belly, shoulders, and cleavage. Jewelry shouldn't jangle. Shoes should cover the toes and be suitable for walking long distances comfortably.

The day of the interview

☐ You might be too nervous to eat breakfast. For an in-person interview pack a small bottle of water and a protein bar. Some interviews can take all day. It's okay to ask for a bathroom break if you need one. If you start to get lightheaded from hunger, use your bathroom break to wolf down your protein bar.

☐ If you're prone to headaches, take a nonprescription headache remedy like naproxen or ibuprofen before you go. Bring some with you as well.

☐ Make sure you're clean, showered, and deodorized, but don't wear fragrance. Some people are sensitive to strong scents, and leaving your interviewer gasping for air or breaking out in hives won't help your chances.

☐ Be there (for a physical interview) or ready with your notes and water to drink (for a phone or video interview) 20 minutes early. Career service professionals will tell you that "on time is late." Your interviewers won't care that you got stuck behind the traffic accident of the century, or that you just reinstalled your operating system.

If you're not there when they expect you, you've lost the job.

☐ When you first meet your interviewer smile, make direct eye contact, and give a brief but firm handshake.

☐ Act like you are happy to be there and excited about meeting everyone and finding out more about the company.

☐ Don't sit until your interviewer invites you to sit.

☐ Never interrupt your interviewer.

☐ Your interviewer is not supposed to ask about your age, marital status, sexual orientation, age, race, religion, or current or future pregnancies. They shouldn't even ask you what year you graduated or whether you want to know about the school district.

☐ **Some interviewers will ask illegal questions anyway.** It's up to you how to respond. You can answer the question; you can give the answer to the question you think they're really asking ("it sounds like you're looking for someone who can work after 5pm. I am able to work after-hours whenever needed."); or you can pretend to mishear and change the subject.

☐ Make sure to confirm each interviewer's name and ask for a business card. This will make you seem engaged and will help you to write your thank-you notes afterwards.

After the interview

As soon as you get home, record the details of your interview on your spreadsheet or on **JibberJobber.com**.

As soon as you get home, send a personal

thank-you note to

everyone who

interviewed you.

A SAMPLE THANK-YOU NOTE

Dear Dr. Lizardo [make sure to use the recipient's preferred title],

Thank you for the opportunity to interview with Yoyodyne Propulsion Systems. Speaking with you last Wednesday has confirmed my desire to join the Yoyodyne team. I really appreciated learning more about the Pocket Overthruster project and am eager to be a part of your new Consumer Devices Division. Please do not hesitate to contact me if you have any further questions.

Sincerely,
Penny Priddy
Penny.Priddy@gmail.com

9. MAKE YOURSELF FIRE-RESISTANT

Libraries have been written on how to be successful in the workplace, so we will just hit a few high points here.

STAY OFF YOUR PHONE DURING WORK HOURS.

Employers complain about new hires who can't stay off their phones. Reserve texting, checking email, or playing a game for when you're not in the company of your boss or colleagues. Search "fired for texting" to get an idea of how people are discussing this issue.

> CONFORM in Speech and Dress and Thought, and You'll Get Promoted When You Ought. Speak the Truth and Have Your Say, and You'll Get Two Weeks' Severance Pay.
>
> A USEFUL WORKPLACE RHYME

CONFORM. Work is not the place to "be yourself." Nonconformity is generally frowned upon in any workplace. Offenses can include dressing too fashionably or not fashionably enough, having hobbies and interests that are too elitist, too low-class, or too weird, working too hard or not working hard enough, having different speech patterns, being in the minority regarding race, gender, age, ability, or body size, or being single when everyone else is married or vice versa.

Not all of these are under your control, and in a just world you wouldn't have to worry about them. But being different does make you stand out, and **if you don't fit in, expect to be held to higher standards than others**.

Consider the case of two coworkers who carpooled to work and walked through the door at the same time every morning. Sometimes they were on time, and other times they were one or two minutes late.

One day one of them was called into the boss's office. She was written up for lateness, put on a performance improvement plan, bumped to a lower pay band, and told she would have to punch a time clock that the boss had procured and placed on her desk. Her coworker—who had been equally tardy—suffered no consequences. In fact, he was amazed and horrified for her [102].

The two employees worked in the same area and had similar job descriptions. But the one who didn't fit in—a woman in a female-unfriendly engineering company—was singled out for discipline. Employees who don't fit in have less room for error. Is this fair? No. Does it really happen? All the time [103]. So what can you do? Fit in to the extent that you can, and don't give your detractors any ammunition.

STAY SAFE- CONFORM

☐ Dress like everyone else (or at least don't look so different that you stand out).

☐ Keep quiet about any unconventional hobbies (some workplace cultures frown on all hobbies, as they occupy time that might be spent working).

☐ Use the same vocabulary, and speak at the same grade level, as your boss.

☐ Come in early [104] and put in a full day's work even if others don't.

☐ Never talk about how you work harder than everyone else.

☐ If you're invited to lunch, accept, but bring your own car so you won't be late getting back to the office.

☐ Participate in work-social activities, even if you would rather not.

☐ If you must leave your desk, inform the secretary (if appropriate) and leave a note ("in design meeting, back by 2pm"). You'd think people might have better things to do than complain to management because you weren't at your desk the one time they came by. You would be wrong.

THE QUICKEST WAY TO GET FIRED: INSUBORDINATION.

In school, you are mostly judged on your individual accomplishments relative to some objective standard. Skipping an assignment isn't fatal. Maybe your grade will take a hit, but missing one deadline won't generally get you kicked out of school.

The workplace is different. At work, it's not about your wonderful, original achievements. It's about keeping systems running and customers happy. Your responsibilities might not make sense to you, and the company's processes might seem antiquated. But this is not the time to show off your brilliance by telling your bosses how stupid their processes are.

At work, refusing an assignment isn't like skipping a reflection paper. **You can get fired for not doing what your boss tells you to.** It's called insubordination.

This may seem horribly unfair. You were hired for your smarts. Organizations are full of inefficiencies, and it doesn't seem right that anyone, least of all yourself, should waste time on poorly-designed processes or projects.

The problem is, it's not up to the new

employee to decide how things get done. Maybe a few changes could make things more efficient or profitable. But if you suggest an improvement and your boss says, "That's great, now do it the way I told you," do it the way your boss told you.

It may be that your bosses are greedy or incompetent. But if they are, you can be sure someone already knows about it and has decided not to do anything about it. Are you, the new hire, going to make things right? A more benign possibility is that processes are the way they are because of laws, contracts, accreditation requirements, or legacy software.

If things really are bad—if you're being asked to do something illegal, or you're getting stuck with menial or low-visibility jobs while your coworkers get the plum assignments—then it's time to start looking for another job.

STAY OUT OF TROUBLE

Be kind, thoughtful, teachable, and adaptable. Before you say anything, **ask yourself: Could this make me look like a know-it-all, a bigot, or that person who thinks the rules don't apply to them?** Be very careful about putting things in writing, especially jokes. Without nonverbal cues, a written message that was meant as lighthearted or sarcastic can come off as offensive.

Except for handshakes, **don't initiate touching anyone.** Some people or cultures are more "huggy" than others, so you can and should accept hugs if they're part of the normal workplace interaction.

Your coworkers may try to recruit you into taking sides in an ongoing feud. Don't let yourself get pulled in. If someone's breaking the law or doing something egregious, report it quietly to law enforcement and/or HR. If what they're doing is not dangerous or destructive to others, stay out of it.

Avoid political discussions at work. If someone tries to draw you into a debate, resist the temptation to point out how wrong they are. Smile politely, claim you don't know much about the issue, and be on your way as quickly as you can.

Somewhere offsite, document all the good

things that you have done so you can include them in future resumes and cover letters and remind your boss of them shortly before review time.

You should also document instances of discrimination, harassment, or illegal or unethical activity—including names, dates, location, and possible witnesses—in the unfortunate event that you might have to make a complaint to HR or consult a lawyer.

10. A GOOD LIFE, NOT A DREAM JOB

You don't have to abandon your dreams. But you should let go of the idea that there is only one dream job out there that will make you happy, and if you don't write the Great American Novel and hit the #1 spot on the New York Time Bestseller List (for example) then life is not worth living. The idea that you have to be SO PASSIONATE ABOUT YOUR JOB

NO, YOU CAN'T BE AN ASTRONAUT

THAT YOU NEVER EVEN WANT TO GO HOME AT NIGHT is a destructive myth that makes people feel inadequate and guilty [105].

Even dream jobs have their not-so-dreamy parts. Writers deal with mean reviews [106], an unsteady publishing industry [107], and an indifferent reading public [108]. Athletes risk life-changing, irreversible injuries [109]. Astronauts have to prepare for zero gravity in a whirling contraption nicknamed the Vomit Comet [110].

WORK PROMOTES CONFIDENCE

WORKS PROGRESS ADMINISTRATION

Jim Bird of **WorkLifeBalance.com** says you don't have to be passionate about your job, but you can take pleasure in *doing* a great job. And you can derive fulfillment from other parts of your life, like your family, friends, pets, hobbies, and creative endeavors.

WILL YOU EVER BE HAPPY?

How do you feel about the following:

1. Your city
2. Your residence
3. The neighbors you have
4. The high school you attended
5. The climate where you live
6. The movies produced today
7. The quality of food you buy
8. Today's cars
9. The local paper
10. Your relaxation time
11. Your first name
12. The people you know
13. Television programs
14. Local speed limits
15. The way people drive
16. Advertising
17. The way you were raised
18. Phone service
19. Public transportation
20. Restaurant food
21. Yourself
22. Modern art
23. Popular music
24. 8½ x 11 paper
25. Your telephone number

This list is called the **Neutral Objects Satisfaction Questionnaire**. Studies show that people who are generally satisfied with the objects listed above are also likely to be satisfied with their jobs, while those who are dissatisfied with everything around them also tend to be dissatisfied with their work [111].

Your job does matter, of course. A great job can boost your well-being, and a miserable workplace can make your life feel like a chore. But people do seem to have a baseline level of happiness. Happiness in adolescence is a good predictor of happiness in adulthood [112], and around fifty percent of baseline happiness is inherited (if you're a natural grump, that's one more thing you can blame on your parents). Aside from your DNA, what determines your happiness are your circumstances, and your "happiness-relevant activities and practices" [113].

Here are some tips you can use to increase your happiness and well-being:

- ☐ Engage in kindness and gratitude. Some ways you can do this are writing letters expressing gratitude, counting your blessings, and performing acts of kindness for others [113].

- ☐ Spend time outdoors [114].

- ☐ Get physical exercise [115].

- ☐ Get enough sleep. Arrange your sleep hours so you wake up naturally, without needing an alarm [116, 117].

- ☐ Spend time with your friends and family. A good social life brings as much happiness as an extra $130,000 per year [118].

☐ Quit smoking and get regular checkups. Good health is worth nearly half a million dollars a year in happiness [118].

☐ While some people enjoy driving, commuting can be stressful [119]; it might be worth it to spend the extra money to move closer to your workplace.

☐ Keep your home and your work space neat enough that you can find what you need when you need it. Clutter can lead to the unpleasant sense that your house isn't really your home [120].

These practices, combined with a job you can stand, can add up to a pretty nice life. You may even have enough spare time to...try out your dreams.

TAKE YOUR DREAM UP FOR A TEST FLIGHT

Kristen Ridout quit her administrative job

to pursue broadcast journalism.

She started in small, remote markets and moved often. But the economics of the industry caught up with her.

> *While I commuted 45 minutes along mountainous roads at four in the morning to report the news, the opportunities for raises and promotions faded away. Two years of doing everything I could to move up in the company were proving fruitless.*

She changed industries when pursuing her dream was no longer sustainable.

> *I don't regret following my dreams to become a journalist, because I would have been unhappy had I not given it a try. I also don't regret throwing in*

the towel after five years,
because I tried my best. [121]

Sometimes your dreams are based on incomplete information. You may have dreamed of living in a big city, but once you get there, you find you can't stand the noise, crowds, and high cost of living. You may start your own business because you want to set your hours and be your own boss, only to find that you can't take a day off, it's impossible to find employees as dedicated as you are, and every one of your customers thinks they're your boss.

You can change course, and you can keep your dream career as a hobby. You might even enjoy it more without the pressure of trying to make it cover your living expenses. Many people have ordinary day jobs and in their nonwork time enjoy singing, playing music, acting, or writing novels.

And once in a while, **a hobby really can turn into a dream job**.

Tess Gerritsen writes the bestselling *Rizzoli & Isles* medical thrillers. But she was a medical doctor first. Elle Boon, Jana DeLeon, and Joanna Penn all quit their corporate jobs to pursue successful writing careers. It can happen. But like Kristen Ridout, you have to set your limits, and know when to quit.

You don't have to choose between throwing aside money and security to pursue your passion versus grinding away at a soul-sucking desk job. You can **choose to build financial security**, which will give you the freedom to pursue your dreams on the side.

Only you can decide how much security you need, how much risk you can live with, and how you want to spend your time and your life. If you're married or partnered, and one of you is pursuing a long-shot career (novelist, entrepreneur, tenure-track humanities professor), you must listen to each other, stay informed, keep talking, and go to counseling if necessary.

Take care of your body; it's the life-support system for your brain.

Reject envy; appreciate the talents of others as a gift to the world. This is harder than it may seem. Our system depends on covetousness and discontent. Envy fuels consumer spending [122], and U.S. consumers power the economy—for now at least [123]. But as much as you can, adopt the attitude of a sports fan, whose pleasure in an athlete's achievement is unmarred by jealousy. Enjoy watching a spacewalk even if you're not the one floating hundreds of miles above the earth.

Kindness is crucial. Be good to those around you and kind to yourself. Invest in activities and attitudes that will keep you too engaged to have time to envy others, and will bring you satisfaction in the long run.

FURTHER READING

Barry, D. (1986). Claw Your Way to the Top: How to Become the Head of a Major Corporation in Roughly a Week. Rodale.

Carnegie, D. (1981). How to win friends and influence people. Simon and Schuster.

Ehrenreich, B. (2010). Nickel and dimed: On (not) getting by in America. Metropolitan Books.

Groening, M. (1987). Work is hell: a cartoon book. WH Allen.

Reardon, K. K. (2002). The secret handshake: Mastering the politics of the business inner circle. Broadway Business.

Sutton, R. I. (2007). The no asshole rule: Building a civilized workplace and surviving one that isn't. Hachette UK.

ABOUT THE AUTHOR

Patience Fairweather is a professor of management who researches and teaches in the areas of entrepreneurship, stereotypes, organizational behavior, and career development. Dr. Fairweather writes under a pen name because her real name is apparently impossible to spell correctly. She has nothing against people following their dreams, as long as they know what they're getting into. Stay in touch at **noyoucantbeanastronaut.com.**

REFERENCES

1. Charette, R.N., *The STEM crisis is a myth.* IEEE Spectrum, 2013. **50**(9): p. 44-59.

2. Casselman, B. *The Economic Guide To Picking A College Major.* FiveThirtyEight.com, 2014.

3. Williams, J.C., et al., *Stable scheduling increases productivity and sales: The Stable Scheduling Study.* University of California Hastings College of the Law, University of Chicago School of Social Service Administration, University of California Kenan-Flagler Business School, 2018.

4. Kizilcec, R., D. Davis, and E. Wang, *Online degree stigma and stereotypes: A new instrument and implications for diversity in higher education.* Available at SSRN 3339768, 2019.

5. Lennon, C., *How Do Online Degrees Affect Labor Market Prospects? Evidence From A Correspondence Audit*

Study. 2019.

6. Federal Reserve Bank of New York. *The Labor Market for Recent College Graduates*. 2019 August 10, 2019 [cited 2019 August 10]; Available from: https://www.newyorkfed.org/research/college-labor-market/college-labor-market_underemployment_rates.html.

7. Camilli, G. and R. Hira, *Introduction to Special Issue—STEM Workforce: STEM Education and the Post-Scientific Society.* Journal of Science Education and Technology, 2019. **28**(1): p. 1-8.

8. Salzman, H. and B. Lieff Benderly, *STEM Performance and Supply: Assessing the Evidence for Education Policy.* Journal of Science Education and Technology, 2019. **28**(1): p. 9-25.

9. National Center for Education Statistics, *Rates of high school completion and bachelor's degree attainment among persons age 25 and over, by race/ethnicity and sex: Selected years, 1910 through 2015.* 2015.

10. Duncan, A., *Toward a new focus on outcomes in higher education.* Speech at

the University of Maryland-Baltimore County, July, 2015. **27**.

11.   U.S. Department of Education, *New State-by-State College Attainment Numbers Show Progress Toward 2020 Goal*. 2012.

12.   Carnevale, A.P. and S.J. Rose, *The Undereducated American.* Georgetown University Center on Education and the Workforce, 2011.

13.   Barnichon, R. and Y. Zylberberg, *Underemployment and the Trickle-Down of Unemployment.* American Economic Journal: Macroeconomics, 2019. **11**(2): p. 40-78.

14.   Howell, D.R. and A.L. Kallenberg, *Declining Job Quality in the United States: Explanations and Evidence.* RSF: The Russell Sage Foundation Journal of the Social Sciences, 2020(forthcoming).

15.   Carnevale, A.P., N. Smith, and J. Strohl, *Help wanted: Projections of job and education requirements through 2018.* 2010: Lumina Foundation.

16.   Richards, E. and D. Terkanian, *Occupational employment projections to*

2022, in *Monthly Labor Review*, U.S.B.o.L. Statistics, Editor. 2013.

17. Bureau of Labor Statistics. *Employment, wages, and projected change in employment by typical entry-level education.* 2019 [cited 2019; Available from: https://www.bls.gov/emp/tables/education-summary.htm.

18. Cappelli, P.H., *Skill gaps, skill shortages, and skill mismatches: Evidence and arguments for the United States.* ILR Review, 2015. **68**(2): p. 251-290.

19. Bruenig, M., *Why Education Does Not Fix Poverty*, in *Policyshop*. 2015, Demos.

20. Government Accountability Office, *LOW-WAGE WORKERS: Poverty and Use of Selected Federal Social Safety Net Programs Persist among Working Families.* 2017.

21. Harrington, P.E. and A.M. Sum, *College Labor Shortages in 2018?* New England Journal of Higher Education, 2010.

22. Hall, J.V. and A.B. Krueger, *An analysis of the labor market for Uber's driver-partners in the United States.* 2016,

National Bureau of Economic Research.
23. Georgetown University Center on Education and the Workforce. *FAQs.* 2017 [cited 2017; Available from: https://cew.georgetown.edu/about-the-center/faqs/.
24. Lumina Foundation for Education, *Grant Database.* 2019.
25. Loonin, D. and J. Margetta Morgan, *Aiming Higher: Looking Beyond Completion to Restore the Promise of Higher Education.* Available at SSRN 3349800, 2019.
26. Education, L.F.f. *Lumina's Goal.* 2019; Available from: https://www.luminafoundation.org/lumina-goal.
27. *The SAGE Encyclopedia of Online Education.* 2016, SAGE Publications, Inc.: Thousand Oaks
Thousand Oaks,, California.
28. Huber, M.T., *Is College for Everyone?* Change: The Magazine of Higher Learning, 2017. **49**(1): p. 7-13.
29. Hirsch, F., *Social limits to growth.* 2005: Routledge.

30. Carlsson, F., O. Johansson-Stenman, and P. Martinsson, *Do you enjoy having more than others? Survey evidence of positional goods.* Economica, 2007. **74**(296): p. 586-598.

31. Stark, E. and P. Poppler, *What are they thinking? Employers requiring college degrees for low-skilled jobs.* SAM Advanced Management Journal, 2016. **81**(3): p. 17-27.

32. Webber, D.A., *Are college costs worth it? How ability, major, and debt affect the returns to schooling.* Economics of Education Review, 2016. **53**: p. 296-310.

33. Tigar, L. *The worst career advice, according to 6 life coaches.* theladders.com, 2017.

34. Flood, A., *Most writers earn less than £600 a year, survey reveals*, in *The Guardian*. 2014.

35. Kerr-Dineen, L., *Here are your odds of becoming a professional athlete (they're not good)*, in *USAToday.com*. 2016.

36. Mann, A., *Your Odds of Becoming an Astronaut Are Going Up*, in *Wired*. 2013, Conde Nast.

37. onlinecasino.ca. *The Odds of Success.* 2017; Available from: https://www.onlinecasino.ca/odds-of-success.

38. Voelck, J., *Directive and Connective:Gender-Based Differences in the Management Styles of Academic Library Managers.* Libraries and the Academy, 2003. **3**(3): p. 393-418.

39. Holland, J.L., *Exploring careers with a typology: What we have learned and some new directions.* American Psychologist, 1996. **51**(4): p. 397.

40. California State University East Bay Academic Advising & Career Education. 2017 [cited 2017; Available from: http://www.csueastbay.edu/aace/major-exploration/riasec-codes.html

41. Van Rooy, D.L. and C. Viswesvaran, *Emotional intelligence: A meta-analytic investigation of predictive validity and nomological net.* Journal of vocational Behavior, 2004. **65**(1): p. 71-95.

42. Cherniss, C., *The business case for emotional intelligence.* Consortium for Research on Emotional Intelligence in

Organizations, 1999. **4**.

43. Lam, L.T. and S.L. Kirby, *Is emotional intelligence an advantage? An exploration of the impact of emotional and general intelligence on individual performance.* The journal of social Psychology, 2002. **142**(1): p. 133-143.

44. Rode, J.C., et al., *A time-lagged study of emotional intelligence and salary.* Journal of Vocational Behavior, 2017. **101**: p. 77-89.

45. Cote, S. and C.T. Miners, *Emotional intelligence, cognitive intelligence, and job performance.* Administrative Science Quarterly, 2006. **51**(1): p. 1-28.

46. Killgore, W.D., et al., *Emotional intelligence is associated with connectivity within and between resting state networks.* Social Cognitive and Affective Neuroscience, 2017. **12**(10): p. 1624-1636.

47. Killgore, W.D., *Self-reported sleep correlates with prefrontal-amygdala functional connectivity and emotional functioning.* Sleep, 2013. **36**(11): p. 1597-1608.

48. Porras, J.I. and B. Anderson, *Improving managerial effectiveness through modeling-based training.* Organizational Dynamics, 1981. **9**(4): p. 60-77.

49. Pescuric, A. and W.C. Byham, *The new look of behavior modeling.* Training & Development, 1996. **50**(7): p. 24-31.

50. Nafukho, F.M., et al., *Developing Emotional Intelligence Skills among Practicing Leaders: Reality or Myth?* Performance Improvement Quarterly, 2016. **29**(1): p. 71-87.

51. Wilkins, M.M., *Signs That You Lack Emotional Intelligence*, in *Harvard Business Review*. 2014.

52. U.S. Office of Personnel Management. *Emotional Intelligence Tests*. Assessment & Selection 2017; Available from: https://www.opm.gov/policy-data-oversight/assessment-and-selection/other-assessment-methods/emotional-intelligence-tests/.

53. Kelly, K.R. and H. Jugovic, *Concurrent validity of the online version of the Keirsey Temperament Sorter II.* Journal of Career Assessment, 2001. **9**(1): p. 49-

59.

54. Myers, I.B., *Introduction to type®*. 1998: CPP.

55. Larson, L.M., P.J. Rottinghaus, and F.H. Borgen, *Meta-analyses of Big Six interests and Big Five personality factors.* Journal of Vocational Behavior, 2002. **61**(2): p. 217-239.

56. Pittenger, D.J., *Cautionary comments regarding the Myers-Briggs Type Indicator.* Consulting Psychology Journal: Practice and Research, 2005. **57**(3): p. 210.

57. Hughes, D.J., et al., *Using personality questionnaires for selection.* The Wiley Blackwell handbook of the psychology of recruitment, selection & retention. Chichester: Wiley-Blackwell, 2017.

58. Saunders, F.W., *Katharine and Isabel: Mother's light, daughter's journey.* 1991: Nicholas Brealey Publishing.

59. Culp, G. and A. Smith, *Understanding psychological type to improve project team performance.* Journal of Management in Engineering, 2001. **17**(1): p. 24-33.

60. De Frum, F., *Personality and interests as predictors of educational streaming and achievement.* 1996.

61. Gale, C.R., et al., *When is higher neuroticism protective against death? Findings from UK Biobank.* Psychological science, 2017. **28**(9): p. 1345-1357.

62. Martin, C.C., *Healthier Without Knowing It: Healthy Neuroticism Does Not Predict Self-Rated Health.* 2016.

63. Perkins, A.M. and P.J. Corr, *Can worriers be winners? The association between worrying and job performance.* Personality and Individual Differences, 2005. **38**(1): p. 25-31.

64. Barrick, M.R. and M.K. Mount, *Select on conscientiousness and emotional stability,* in *Handbook of Principles of Organizational Behavior,* E.A. Locke, Editor. 2004, Blackwell: Malden, MA. p. 15-28.

65. Borman, W.C., et al., *Personality Predictors of Citizenship Performance.* International Journal of Selection and Assessment, 2001. **9**(1-2): p. 52-69.

66. Avis, J.M., J.D. Kudisch, and V.J.

Fortunato, *Examining the incremental validity and adverse impact of cognitive ability and conscientiousness on job performance.* Journal of Business and Psychology, 2002. **17**(1): p. 87-105.

67. Boyce, C.J., A.M. Wood, and G.D.A. Brown, *The dark side of conscientiousness: Conscientious people experience greater drops in life satisfaction following unemployment.* Journal of Research in Personality, 2010. **44**(4): p. 535-539.

68. Dahm, A.-S., et al., *The burden of conscientiousness? Examining brain activation and cortisol response during social evaluative stress.* Psychoneuroendocrinology, 2017. **78**(Supplement C): p. 48-56.

69. Gosling, S.D., P.J. Rentfrow, and W.B. Swann, *A very brief measure of the Big-Five personality domains.* Journal of Research in personality, 2003. **37**(6): p. 504-528.

70. Walsemann, K.M., B.A. Bell, and R.A. Hummer, *Effects of Timing and Level of Degree Attained on Depressive*

Symptoms and Self-Rated Health at Midlife. American Journal of Public Health, 2012. **102**(3): p. 557-563.

71. Ma, J., et al., *State-level educational disparities in mortality in the United States, 2010-2014.* Preventive medicine, 2017.

72. Ma, J., M. Pender, and M. Welch, *Education Pays 2016: The Benefits of Higher Education for Individuals and Society. Trends in Higher Education Series.* College Board, 2016.

73. Ost, B., W. Pan, and D.A. Webber, *The Returns to College Persistence for Marginal Students: Regression Discontinuity Evidence from University Dismissal Policies.* 2016.

74. Giani, M.S., P. Attewell, and D. Walling, *The Value of an Incomplete Degree: Heterogeneity in the Labor Market Benefits of College Non-Completion.* The Journal of Higher Education, 2019: p. 1-26.

75. Huo, H., J. Redford, and J. Ralph, *Stats in Brief.* 2019.

76. Webber, D.A., *Projected Lifetime*

Earnings for Bachelor's Degree Holders by Major. Chemical Engineering, 2018. **3**(2,861,315): p. 4,138,457.

77. Eide, E.R., M.J. Hilmer, and M.H. Showalter, *Is it where you go or what you study? The relative influence of college selectivity and college major on earnings.* Contemporary Economic Policy, 2016. **34**(1): p. 37-46.

78. Hein, V., B. Smerdon, and M. Sambolt, *Predictors of Postsecondary Success.* College and Career Readiness and Success Center, 2013.

79. Bartik, T.J. and B. Hershbein, *Degrees of poverty: The relationship between family income background and the returns to education.* 2018.

80. Abel, J.R. and R. Deitz, *College may not pay off for everyone.* Liberty Street Economics, Federal Reserve Bank of New York, 2014.

81. Hersh, R.H., *Intention and Perceptions A National Survey of Public Attitudes Toward Liberal Arts Education.* Change: The Magazine of Higher Learning, 1997. **29**(2): p. 16-23.

82.   Bradforth, S.E., et al., *University learning: Improve undergraduate science education.* Nature News, 2015. **523**(7560): p. 282.

83.   Bettinger, E.P. and B.T. Long, *Mass Instruction or Higher Learning? The Impact of College Class Size on Student Retention and Graduation.* Education Finance and Policy, 2016.

84.   Cellini, S.R. and N. Turner, *Gainfully Employed? Assessing the Employment and Earnings of For-Profit College Students Using Administrative Data.* 2016, National Bureau of Economic Research.

85.   Armona, L., R. Chakrabarti, and M. Lovenheim, *How does for-profit college attendance affect student loans, defaults, and earnings?* 2017.

86.   Snider, S., *The 25 Highest-Paying Jobs That Don't Require a College Degree,* in *U.S. News* 2017.

87.   Tai, R.H., P.M. Sadler, and J.J. Mintzes, *Factors influencing college science success.* Journal of College Science Teaching, 2006. **36**(1): p. 52.

88. Tyson, W., *Modeling engineering degree attainment using high school and college physics and calculus coursetaking and achievement.* Journal of Engineering Education, 2011. **100**(4): p. 760-777.

89. Cornelius, L.M. and S.A. Frank, *Perspectives on Student Loan Debt Levels: Student Loan Debt Levels and Their Implications for Borrowers, Society, and the Economy.* Educational Considerations, 2015. **42**(2): p. 5.

90. Scott-Clayton, J.E., *What accounts for gaps in student loan default, and what happens after.* 2018.

91. Addo, F.R., *Parents' Wealth Helps Explain Racial Disparities in Student Loan Debt.* In the Balance, 2018(19): p. 1-3.

92. Rivera, L.A., *Pedigree: How elite students get elite jobs.* 2016: Princeton University Press.

93. Bruni, F., *Where You Go Is Not Who You'll Be: An Antidote to the College Admissions Mania.* 2015: Grand Central Publishing.

94. Executive Office of the President of the United States, *USING FEDERAL DATA TO MEASURE AND IMPROVE THE PERFORMANCE OF U.S. INSTITUTIONS OF HIGHER EDUCATION.* 2017.

95. Ray, J. and S. Kafka, *Life in college matters for life after college.* Life, 2014. **5**.

96. Silva, E. and T. White, *The Carnegie unit: Past, present, and future.* Change: The Magazine of Higher Learning, 2015. **47**(2): p. 68-72.

97. Drouin, M., et al., *Facebook fired: Legal perspectives and young adults' opinions on the use of social media in hiring and firing decisions.* Computers in Human Behavior, 2015. **46**: p. 123-128.

98. Warren, C., *10 People Who Lost Jobs Over Social Media Mistakes*, in *Mashable.com.* 2011.

99. *Elonis v. US*, in *S. Ct.* 2015, Supreme Court. p. 2001.

100. Curran, D., *Are you ready? Here is all the data Facebook and Google have on you.* The Guardian, 2018. **30**.

101. Waung, M., et al., *Impression*

Management Use in Resumes and Cover Letters. Journal of Business and Psychology, 2017. **32**(6): p. 727-746.

102. Eipper, C., *The Ruling Trinity: A Community Study of Church, State and Business in Ireland.* 1986, Brookfield, VT: Gower.

103. Gaines, J., *Women in Male-Dominated Careers.* Women, 2017. **5**: p. 3-2017.

104. Yam, K.C., R. Fehr, and C.M. Barnes, *Morning employees are perceived as better employees: Employees' start times influence supervisor performance ratings.* Journal of Applied Psychology, 2014. **99**(6): p. 1288-1299.

105. Levy, J., *The Dream Job Is a Myth. Focus Instead on Living Your Best Life.*, in *Entrepreneur.* 2017.

106. *One-Star Book Reviews.* 2017; Available from: http://onestarbookreview.tumblr.com/.

107. Horne, A., *Publishing: the last (and next?) five years.* The Indexer, 2017. **35**(1): p. 2-9.

108. Perrin, A., *Who doesn't read books in America.* Pew Research Center, 2016.

18.

109. Iverson, G.L., *Chronic traumatic encephalopathy and risk of suicide in former athletes.* Br J Sports Med, 2014. **48**(2): p. 162-164.

110. Dempsey, R., et al., *Thank you for flying the vomit comet.* The Physics Teacher, 2007. **45**(2): p. 75-79.

111. Judge, T.A. and C.L. Hulin, *Job satisfaction as a reflection of disposition: A multiple source causal analysis.* Organizational Behavior and Human Decision Processes, 1993. **56**(3): p. 388-421.

112. Staw, B., N. E. Bell, and J. A. Clausen, *The Dispositional Approach To Job Attitudes: A Lifetime Longitudinal Test.* Vol. 31. 1986. 56.

113. Lyubomirsky, S., K.M. Sheldon, and D. Schkade, *Pursuing happiness: The architecture of sustainable change.* Review of general psychology, 2005. **9**(2): p. 111.

114. MacKerron, G. and S. Mourato, *Happiness is greater in natural environments.* Global Environmental

Change, 2013. **23**(5): p. 992-1000.

115. Lubans, D., et al., *Physical activity for cognitive and mental health in youth: A systematic review of mechanisms.* Pediatrics, 2016: p. e20161642.

116. Kripke, D.F., et al., *Mortality associated with sleep duration and insomnia.* Archives of general psychiatry, 2002. **59**(2): p. 131-136.

117. Ong, A.D., et al., *Positive affect and sleep: A systematic review.* Sleep medicine reviews, 2017. **35**: p. 21-32.

118. Powdthavee, N., *Putting a price tag on friends, relatives, and neighbours: Using surveys of life satisfaction to value social relationships.* The Journal of Socio-Economics, 2008. **37**(4): p. 1459-1480.

119. Novaco, R.W. and O.I. Gonzalez, *Commuting and well-being.* Technology and well-being, 2009. **3**: p. 174-4.

120. Roster, C.A., J.R. Ferrari, and M.P. Jurkat, *The dark side of home: Assessing possession 'clutter'on subjective well-being.* Journal of Environmental Psychology, 2016. **46**: p. 32-41.

121. Ridout, K., *Reality Check: I Left My*

Dream Job To Be More Practical, in *Entrepreneur.com*. 2015, Entrepreneur Media.

122. Wooten, D.B., R.L. Harrison, and N. Mitchell, *Benign envy: is there a dark side of light green?* AMS review, 2011. **1**(3-4): p. 137-139.

123. Emmons, W.R. *Don't expect consumer spending to be the engine of economic growth it once was*. Regional Economist: Insights on economic issues in today's headlines, 2012.

www.ingramcontent.com/pod-product-compliance
Lightning Source LLC
Chambersburg PA
CBHW030521100426
42813CB00001B/109